SO-AAN-338

SPECTRUM®

Critical Thinking for Math

Grade 5

Published by Spectrum®
an imprint of Carson Dellosa Education
Greensboro, NC

Spectrum®
An imprint of Carson Dellosa Education
PO Box 35665
Greensboro, NC 27425 USA

© 2017 Carson Dellosa Education. Except as permitted under the United States Copyright Act, no part of this publication may be reproduced, stored, or distributed in any form or by any means (mechanically, electronically, recording, etc.) without the prior written consent of Carson Dellosa Education. Spectrum® is an imprint of Carson Dellosa Education.

Printed in the USA • All rights reserved.

ISBN 978-1-4838-3552-5

03-025217784

Table of Contents Grade 5

Table of Contents, continued

Check What You Know

Multiplying and Dividing Whole Numbers

Multiply or divide.

1. 9435
    × 15

2. 588
    × 204

3. 32)1472

4. 55)3520

Solve the problems below using multiplication or division. Be sure to show your work.

5. A toy store receives 1,023 boxes of toys in a shipment. If there are 32 toys in each box, how many toys has the toy store received?

6. Marcus needs at least 1,000 juice boxes for his after-school program. The juice boxes come in packs of 12. How many juice box packs does Marcus need to buy?

Lesson 1.1 Multiplying through 4 Digits

You can use place value to multiply multi-digit numbers.

2135	It can work the opposite	Or use the standard
× 23	way as well:	method:

$$2000 \times 23 = 46000$$
$$100 \times 23 = 2300$$
$$30 \times 23 = 690$$
$$+ \quad 5 \times 23 = 115$$
$$\overline{\qquad 49,105}$$

2135
× 23
$$2135 \times 20 = 42700$$
$$+ \quad 2135 \times 3 = 6405$$
$$\overline{\qquad 49,105}$$

2135
× 23
$$6405$$
$$+ 42700$$
$$\overline{49,105}$$

Solve the problems below using place value. Show your work.

4590
× 321

7832
× 73

3754
× 215

5614
× 91

Lesson 1.2 Multi-Digit Division Using Arrays

You can use a rectangular array to solve division problems.

13 26 39 52 65 78 91 104 117 130 143 156

$156 \div 13 = ?$

1. Create a column with 13 marks.

2. Continue adding columns with 13 marks until the dividend is reached (156).

3. Count the number of columns to find the quotient (12).
$156 \div 13 = 12$

1   2   3   4   5   6   7   8   9   10   11   12

Create rectangular arrays to solve the division problems.

$184 \div 23 =$

$330 \div 22 =$

Lesson 1.3 Using Long Division

To use long division, decompose the
dividend and divide each part by the divisor
using estimation.

Then, subtract and repeat until you
reach the ones place.

$$
\begin{array}{r}
124 \\
56\overline{)6944} \\
-5600 \\
\hline
1344 \\
-1120 \\
\hline
224 \\
-224 \\
\hline
0
\end{array}
$$

$6900 \div 56 =$ about 100

$1300 \div 56 =$ about 20

$224 \div 56 = 4$

Use long division to solve each problem below. Show your work.

$23\overline{)1955}$

$83\overline{)3901}$

$92\overline{)5796}$

$21\overline{)6825}$

Lesson 1.4 Using Estimation and Area Models to Divide

You can use estimation and area models to solve complicated division problems. Estimate using known multiplication and division facts.

For 768 ÷ 12, you know that 720 is close to 768, so you can use 60 × 12 as a starting point for the area model.

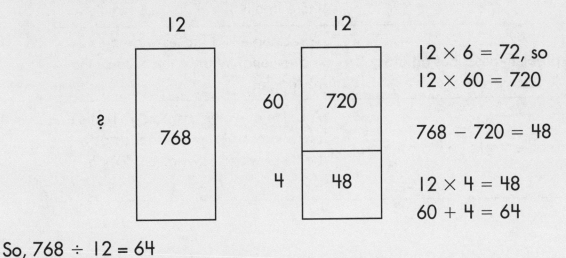

12 × 6 = 72, so
12 × 60 = 720

768 − 720 = 48

12 × 4 = 48
60 + 4 = 64

So, 768 ÷ 12 = 64

Use estimation and area models to solve these division problems. Show your work.

2,408 ÷ 43 =   4,524 ÷ 52 =

Lesson 1.5 Multiplication in the Real World

These clues tell you multiplication can be used to solve a problem.

Clue	Example
The problem describes equal groups.	There are 4 boxes with 8 games in each box. How many games are there in all?
The problem describes an array.	A rectangle is 4 inches wide and 2 inches long. What is the area of the rectangle?
The problem asks you to compare.	A bottle of water costs $2. A bottle of soda costs 2 times as much as a bottle of water. How much does a bottle of soda cost?

Solve each problem. Then, explain why each problem can be solved using multiplication.

The restaurant prepares 65 pizza crusts for every hour they are open on Saturday. If the restaurant is open for 12 hours, how many pizza crusts do they prepare?

_____

_____

An auditorium seats people in 123 rows. If there are 36 seats in each row, how many seats are in the auditorium?

_____

_____

Lesson 1.6   Division in the Real World

These clues tell you division can be used to solve a problem.

Clue	Example
The problem describes equal groups, and the group size or number of groups is unknown.	There are 156 cookies divided equally into 13 bags. How many cookies are in each bag?
The problem describes an array, and the number of rows or columns is unknown.	A room has an area of 225 square feet. If the room is 15 feet long, how wide is the room?
The problem asks you to compare, and the original value or multiplier is unknown.	A video game for a computer costs $10, but a game for a phone costs $2. How many times as much does the computer game cost compared to the phone game?

Solve each problem. Then, explain why each problem can be solved using division.

The school purchased 9,864 books for its fifth graders to take home over the summer. If each student takes home 12 books, how many fifth graders are in the school?

_____

_____

A combination meal with a sandwich, chips, and a drink costs $12. That price is 3 times more than 1 sandwich by itself. How much does just 1 sandwich cost?

_____

_____

Check What You Learned

Multiplying and Dividing Whole Numbers

CHAPTER 1 POSTTEST

Use place value to multiply. Show your work.

1. 8251
   × 64

2. 4183
   × 87

Use the standard algorithm to multiply. Show your work.

3. 6718
   × 19

4. 4722
   × 48

5. 4867
   × 39

Use long division to solve questions 6 and 7. Use estimation and area models to solve question 8.

6. 62)7626

7. 27)1512

8. 48)9744

Check What You Learned

Multiplying and Dividing Whole Numbers

Solve the problems below using multiplication or division. Show your work and tell what clues helped you solve the problem.

9. A manufacturer can make 4,574 pairs of jeans in one hour. If they operate for 14 hours each day, how many pairs of jeans can they make in one day?

They can make _____ pairs of jeans.

What is the clue in this problem? _____

10. The apple orchard has 5,952 apple trees. If the trees are arranged in rows of 96, how many rows of trees are there?

There are _____ rows of trees.

What is the clue in this problem? _____

NAME _____

 ## Check What You Know

Understanding Place Value

Follow the directions for the number.

59<u>5</u>,682

1. Write the number in expanded form.

_____

2. Divide the number by 1,000. Give your answer as a decimal.

_____

3. Compare: 592,682 _____ 591,683

4. Write the place value of the underlined digit.

_____

5. Round the number to the place value of the underlined digit.

_____

6. Write the rounded number as a power of 10 to the nearest one.

_____

Check What You Know

Understanding Place Value

Follow the directions for the number.

58.9<u>2</u>7

7. Write the place value of the underlined digit.

_____

8. Round the number to the place value of the underlined digit.

_____

9. Multiply the number by 100.

_____

10.   Compare: 58.927 _____ 58.94

Order the numbers from least to greatest.

11.   65.48, 6.548, 65.408, 65.485

_____

Lesson 2.1   Identifying Place Value to Millions

Every digit in a number has a value based on its place in the number. For example, in the number 5,239,168, the 9 has a value of 9,000 because it is in the thousands place. A place value table can help you find the value.

millions	hundred thousands	ten thousands	thousands	hundreds	tens	ones
5	2	3	9	1	6	8

Use the place value table to find the value of each underlined digit. Put the values in order on the line below.

7,4<u>8</u>3,312

Value: _____

4,329,6<u>7</u>3

Value: _____

5,94<u>2</u>,691

Value: _____

<u>8</u>,759,267

Value: _____

_____

Lesson 2.2 Identifying Place Value to Thousandths

In the number 4,973.562, the 6 has a value of 6 hundredths, or 0.06, because it is in the hundredths place. A place value table can help you find the value.

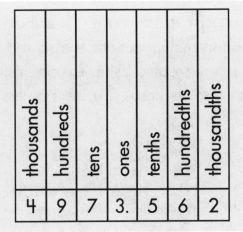

thousands	hundreds	tens	ones	tenths	hundredths	thousandths
4	9	7	3.	5	6	2

Tell the value of each underlined digit by using the place value table. Put the values in order on the line below.

5,689.5̲47

Value: _____

9,4̲89.392

Value: _____

6,289.36̲5

Value: _____

4,392.732̲

Value: _____

Lesson 2.3   Powers of Ten

An **exponent** is a number that shows how many times a base number should be used in multiplication. It also shows how many zeros are in the number. A power of ten is created using exponents. The base number is always 10. Other numbers can also be created using powers of ten.

$10^1 = 1\underline{0} = 10$ $7 \times 10^1 = 70$
$10^2 = 1\underline{0} \times 1\underline{0} = 1\underline{00}$ $7 \times 10^2 = 700$
$10^3 = 1\underline{0} \times 1\underline{0} \times 1\underline{0} = 1,\underline{000}$ $7 \times 10^3 = 7,000$
$10^4 = 1\underline{0} \times 1\underline{0} \times 1\underline{0} \times 1\underline{0} = 1\underline{0,000}$ $7 \times 10^4 = 70,000$

Rewrite each number as a power of ten.

90,000   60,000,000   3,000

_____   _____   _____

Write each power of ten as a number. Compare using **>**, **<**, or **=**.

7×10^4 7×10^5

_____      _____

25×10^5 26×10^5

_____   _____

Lesson 2.4   Expanded Form

A number written in **expanded form** shows the sum of the values of each digit. The number is separated into each of its parts using place value. This is also called **decomposing** a number.

$3,268 = 3,000 + 200 + 60 + 8$

$67,491 = 60,000 + 7,000 + 400 + 90 + 1$

Find the missing value in each expanded-form number.

$695 = 600 +$ _____ $+ 5$

_____ $= 5,000 + 800 + 30 + 6$

$20,376 =$ _____ $+ 300 + 70 + 6$

$500,913 = 500,000 + 900 + 10 +$ _____

_____ $= 900,000 + 50,000 + 4,000 + 200 + 50 + 7$

Lesson 2.5 Comparing and Ordering Decimals

You can compare and order decimal numbers by aligning the decimal point in each value. Then, evaluate each number in comparison with the others.

4.05 ⟶ This value is least. It has a lower value in both decimal places.
4.56 ⟶ This value is second least. It is 0.001 less than 4.561.
4.561 ⟶ This value is second greatest. It is 0.001 more than 4.56.
5.32 ⟶ This value is greatest. It has the greatest value in the ones place.

Place the values below in order from least to greatest. Explain your thinking.

7.82, 8.73, 7.802, 8.729

_____ ⟶ _____ .

_____ ⟶ _____ .

_____ ⟶ _____ .

_____ ⟶ _____ .

5.67, 5.607, 5.671, 5.617

_____ ⟶ _____ .

_____ ⟶ _____ .

_____ ⟶ _____ .

_____ ⟶ _____ .

Lesson 2.5 Rounding Whole Numbers

You can use place value to round whole numbers.

Round 51,927 to the nearest thousand.	Round 324,963 to the nearest ten.
Look at the hundreds digit: 5<u>1</u>,927	Look at the ones digit: 324,9<u>63</u>
9 is greater than or equal to 5, so round 1 to 2 in the thousands place.	3 is less than 5, so leave 6 the same in the tens place.
52,000	324,960

Round each number to the underlined place. Explain your work.

89,<u>3</u>46 _____

_____ is _____ 5, so _____ .

1<u>1</u>5,332 _____

_____ is _____ 5, so _____ .

<u>2</u>18,416 _____

_____ is _____ 5, so _____ .

Lesson 2.6 Rounding Decimals

You can use place value to round numbers with decimals.

Round 3.541 to the nearest hundredth. | Round 7.663 to the nearest tenth.

Look at the thousandths digit: 3.5<u>4</u>1 | Look at the hundredths digit: 7.6<u>6</u>3

1 is less than 5, so leave 4 the same in the hundredths place. | 6 is greater than or equal to 5, so round 6 to 7 in the tenths place.

3.54 | 7.7

Round each number to the underlined place. Explain your work.

5.8<u>4</u>1 _____

_____ is _____ 5, so _____ .

2<u>9</u>.678 _____

_____ is _____ 5, so _____ .

6.<u>5</u>26 _____

_____ is _____ 5, so _____ .

Lesson 2.7 Place Value in Other Systems

Time has a place value system with a base of 60.

I hour = 60 minutes   I minute = 60 seconds

To add or subtract, line the times up based on their place value. Use 60 as the base if regrouping is necessary.

I hour 10 minutes
+ 2 hours 27 minutes

3 hours 37 minutes

$\overset{4}{\cancel{5}}$ minutes $\overset{75}{\cancel{15}}$ seconds
− I minute 30 seconds

3 minutes 45 seconds

Add or subtract. Show your work.

4 min. 24 sec.
+ 2 min. 57 sec.

3 hr. 15 min.
− 2 hr. 20 min.

Show how to add I hour 12 minutes and 10 seconds to 3 hours 4 minutes and 52 seconds using a time-based place value system.

Check What You Learned

Understanding Place Value

Find the value of each underlined digit.

1. 9,42<u>4</u>,201 _____

2. 4,<u>2</u>88.482 _____

Write each power of ten as a number. Use **<**, **>**, or **=** to compare.

3. 34×10^3 35×10^2

_____   ____   _____

4. On the line below, put the four numbers you wrote in questions #1–4 in order from least to greatest.

_____

Rewrite each number as a power of ten to the ones place.

5. 9,700 _____

6. 3,000,000 _____

Find which value is incorrect in each expanded-form number.

7. 23,845 = 2,000 + 3,000 + 800 + 40 + 5 _____

8. 3,840,764 = 3,000,000 + 800,000 + 4,000 + 700 + 60 + 4

_____

Check What You Learned

Understanding Place Value

Order the decimals from least to greatest. Explain your thinking.

9. 8.72, 8.702, 8.721, 8.719

_____ → _____
_____.

_____ → _____
_____.

_____ → _____
_____.

_____ → _____
_____.

Round the number to the underlined place. Explain your work.

10. 95.<u>5</u>92   _____

_____ is _____ 5, so _____.

Solve the problem. Show your work.

11.   4 min. 24 sec.
    + 2 min. 57 sec.

NAME _____

Check What You Know

Using Decimals

Add or subtract.

1. 52.61
    + 32.54
    ———

2. 912.67
    + 427.48
    ———

3. 6.70
    − 3.26
    ———

4. 93.4
    − 36.7
    ———

Multiply or divide.

5. 2.1
    × 9.3
    ———

6. 4.09
    × 6.7
    ———

7. 2.52)‾153.72‾

8. 0.34)‾85‾

Lesson 3.1 Adding Decimals to Hundredths

When adding decimals, align the numbers by place value.

What is 7.5 + 3.24?

Align the numbers.

Add.

7.5 + 3.24 = 10.74

tens	ones	tenths	hundredths
	7.	5	
	3.	2	4
1	0.	7	4

Solve the problems.

43.85 + 21.9

tens	ones	tenths	hundredths
4	3.	8	5
2	1.	9	

9,583.1 + 492.29

ten thousands	thousands	hundreds	tens	ones	tenths	hundredths
	9	5	8	3.	1	
		4	9	2.	2	9

Lesson 3.2   Subtracting Decimals to Hundredths

When subtracting decimals, align the numbers by place value.

What is 8.7 − 4.23?

Align the numbers.

Place zeros if necessary.

Subtract.

8.7 − 4.23 = 4.47

ones	tenths	hundredths
8.	7	0
4.	2	3
4.	4	7

Solve the problems.

4,347.37 − 931.39

thousands	hundreds	tens	ones	tenths	hundredths
4	3	4	7.	3	7
	9	3	1.	3	9

2,934.2 − 1,842.13

thousands	hundreds	tens	ones	tenths	hundredths
2	9	3	4.	2	0
1	8	4	2.	1	3

Lesson 3.3 Multiplying Decimals Using Models

You can use grid systems to multiply decimals. For example, in the problem 0.4 × 0.8, the product is 4 tenths of 8 tenths.

 X  =

When the grids are placed over each other, the overlapping part in green shows the product. In this example, 4 tenths of 8 tenths is 32 hundredths, or 0.32.

Use models to solve the problem below. Then, explain your answer.

0.6 × 0.9 = _____

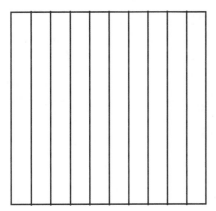 X 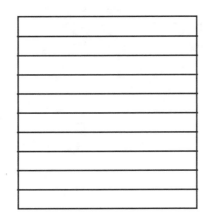 =

_____ tenths of _____ tenths is _____ hundredths or _____.

Lesson 3.4 Dividing Decimals Using Models

You can use grid systems to divide decimals. For example, in the problem 2.4 ÷ 6, the quotient will divide 2.4 into 6 equal portions.

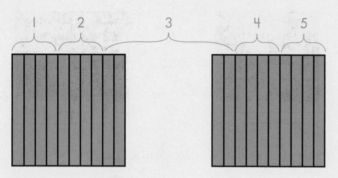 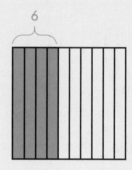

When the grids are divided into equal sections, the size of one section is the quotient. In this example, 2.4 divided into 6 equal portions is 0.4, or 4 tenths.

Draw and label a grid-system model to solve the problem. Explain your answer.

6.4 ÷ 8 = _____

Lesson 3.5 Multiplying Decimals Using Rules

When multiplying decimals, you can look at the number of decimal places in the factors to find out how many decimal places are in the product.

$$
\begin{array}{r}
7.14 \\
\times\ 3.1 \\
\hline
714 \\
+\ 21420 \\
\hline
22.134
\end{array}
$$

2 decimal places
+ 1 decimal place
_____
3 decimal places

1. Multiply.

2. Count decimal places in factors.

3. Count and place decimal in product.

Solve the problems. Tell how many decimal places are in the factors for each problem.

$$
\begin{array}{r}
3.72 \\
\times\ 8.6 \\
\hline
\end{array}
$$

number of decimal places _____

$$
\begin{array}{r}
46.1 \\
\times\ 17 \\
\end{array}
$$

number of decimal places _____

Lesson 3.6 Dividing Decimals Using Rules

When dividing decimals using long division, multiply both the divisor and dividend by a power of ten to eliminate decimal places from the divisor.

$0.13\overline{)1.183}$ = 118.3 ÷ 13 = 9.1

$$0.13\overline{)1.183}$$
$$\times\ 100$$

$$\begin{array}{r} 9.1 \\ 13\overline{)118.3} \\ -117 \\ \hline 13 \\ -13 \\ \hline 0 \end{array}$$

Solve these problems by multiplying the divisor and dividend by a power of ten and working out the long division.

$2.6\overline{)18.798}$ Power of 10 used _____

$3.14\overline{)20.41}$ Power of 10 used _____

Lesson 3.7   Using Decimals in the Real World

Use what you have learned about decimals to solve these multi-step problems. Show your work and tell which operations you used.

If Pete were 13.5 inches taller, he would be twice as tall as Jonathan. If Jonathan is 45.8 inches tall, how tall is Pete?

Which operations did you use? First, I _____. Then, I _____.

Tia bought her dad a new tie for $19.95. Then, she bought her sister a new pair of earrings for $9.38. If she started with $55.00, how much money does she have left?

Which operations did you use? First, I _____. Then, I _____.

NAME _____

 Check What You Learned

Using Decimals

Add or subtract.

1. 4,323.67 + 518.9

thousands	hundreds	tens	ones	tenths	hundredths
4	3	2	3.	6	7
	5	1	8.	9	0

2. 8,583.43 − 276.94

thousands	hundreds	tens	ones	tenths	hundredths
8	5	8	3.	4	3
	2	7	6.	9	4

Use models to solve the problem below. Then, explain your answer.

3. 0.4 × 0.7 = _____

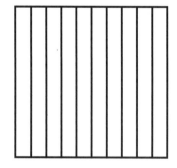 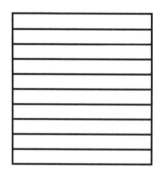 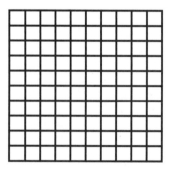

_____ tenths of _____ tenths is _____ hundredths or _____.

CHAPTER 3 POSTTEST

Check What You Learned

Using Decimals

Multiply or divide using rules.

4. 8.56
    × 3.72
    _____

5. 2.52)‾1‾5‾3‾.‾7‾2‾

Solve this multi-step decimal problem. Show your work and explain which operations you used to find your answer.

6. Michael and Michelle are twins. For their birthday, they receive $25.00 from their aunt, $32.55 from their grandmother, and $15.87 from their parents. If the twins split the money evenly, how much money will they each receive?

Which operations did you use? First, I _____ .

Then, I _____ .

Check What You Know

Understanding Fractions

Change improper fractions to mixed numbers and mixed numbers to improper fractions. Show your work.

1. $6\frac{1}{8}$ _____

2. $\frac{53}{6}$ _____

Find the greatest common factor. Show your work.

3. 6, 9, 18 _____

Find the least common multiple. Show your work.

4. 4, 5, 10 _____

5. Put the fraction $\frac{12}{36}$ in simplest form.

Check What You Know

Understanding Fractions

Put these fractions in order from least to greatest. Draw a picture to show your work.

6. $\dfrac{1}{3}$, $\dfrac{1}{2}$, $\dfrac{1}{4}$

Convert each fraction into a decimal. Convert each decimal into a fraction. Show your work.

7. $\dfrac{7}{8}$

8. 1.75

Solve the problem. Draw a picture to show your work.

9. Lou and David order 2 pizzas of the same size for dinner. The pepperoni pizza is sliced into 8 equal pieces, and the cheese pizza is sliced into 12 equal pieces. If Lou eats 5 pieces of pepperoni pizza and David eats 7 pieces of cheese pizza, who has eaten more pizza?

Lesson 4.1 Converting Fractions

You can use multiplication and addition to convert mixed numbers to improper fractions.

$3\frac{1}{4} =$ 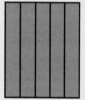  $= \frac{13}{4}$

$$3 \times 4 + 1 = 13$$

You can use division and remainders to convert improper fractions to mixed numbers.

$\frac{8}{5} =$ $= 1\frac{3}{5}$

$$8 \div 5 = 1 \text{ R3}$$

Convert the mixed number to an improper fraction. Convert the improper fraction to a mixed number. Explain how each change was made.

$2\frac{2}{3}$ _____

_____

_____

$\frac{9}{4}$ _____

_____

_____

Lesson 4.2   Number Relationships

When working with fractions, you will often need to find the least common multiple (LCM) and the greatest common factor (GCF) of a set of numbers.

Least Common Multiple

What is the smallest common number that is a multiple of each number?

2: 2, 4, 6, 8, 10, (12)
3: 3, 6, 9, (12)
4: 4, 8, (12)

12 is the LCM. It is the smallest multiple found in all 3 lists.

Greatest Common Factor

What is the highest number that divides exactly into each number?

12: 1, 2, 3, (4) 6, 12
20: 1, 2, (4) 5, 10, 20
32: 1, 2, (4) 8, 16, 32

4 is the GCF. It is the greatest factor found in all 3 lists.

Find the least common multiple by listing multiples.

5:

15:                    LCM is _____.

20:

Find the greatest common factor by listing factors.

9:

18:                    GCF is _____.

12:

Lesson 4.3 Finding Equivalent Fractions

You can use pictures, multiplication, or division to find equivalent fractions. For example, here is how to find equivalent fractions for $\frac{1}{4}$.

$$\bigcirc = \frac{1}{4} \qquad \bigcirc = \frac{2}{8} \qquad \bigcirc = \frac{3}{12}$$

$$\frac{1 \times 2}{4 \times 2} = \frac{2}{8} \quad \text{or} \quad \frac{3 \div 3}{12 \div 3} = \frac{1}{4}$$

List 2 fractions that are equivalent to each fraction shown. Prove the fractions are equivalent using pictures.

Fraction	Equal Fractions	Proof
$\frac{2}{3}$		
$\frac{3}{5}$		

Lesson 4.4 Simplifying Fractions

To simplify a fraction, find the greatest common factor of the numerator and denominator.

$\dfrac{4}{12}$ 4: 1, 2, ④
12: 1, 2, 3, 4, ⑥ 12

$\dfrac{4}{12}$ $\dfrac{\div 4}{\div 4}$ = $\dfrac{1}{3}$

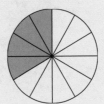

Find the greatest common factor of the numerator and denominator to simplify these fractions.

$\dfrac{6}{30}$ 6:

         30:

$\dfrac{8}{24}$ 8:

         24:

$\dfrac{15}{35}$ 15:

         35:

Lesson 4.5 Comparing and Ordering Fractions

The denominator is a clue about the size of the fraction. If the denominator is larger, the portion that one part of the fraction represents will be smaller.

 $\dfrac{1}{4}$ is greater than $\dfrac{1}{8}$

You can put fractions in order when they have different numerators and denominators. Find the least common multiple of the denominators so the fractions represent equal portions. Then, compare the numerators.

 $\dfrac{2}{5}$ $\dfrac{1}{3}$  $\dfrac{5}{6}$

$$\frac{2}{5} = \frac{12}{30} \qquad \frac{1}{3} = \frac{10}{30} \qquad \frac{5}{6} = \frac{25}{30}$$

$$\frac{10}{30} < \frac{12}{30} < \frac{25}{30} \quad = \quad \frac{1}{3} < \frac{2}{5} < \frac{5}{6}$$

Put the fractions in order from least to greatest. Find the least common multiple of the denominators to tell how many portions you need to compare the fractions.

$\dfrac{1}{4}$, $\dfrac{2}{5}$, $\dfrac{3}{10}$ _____

Lesson 4.6 Changing Fractions to Decimals

You can change fractions into decimals using mathematical operations.

$\frac{1}{4}$

$$1 \div 4 = \quad \begin{array}{r} 0.25 \\ 4\overline{)1.00} \\ -\ 8 \\ \hline 20 \\ -\ 20 \\ \hline 0 \end{array} = 0.25$$

Use division to change these fractions into decimals. Illustrate using the grids.

Fraction	Illustration	Divide	Decimal
$\frac{3}{10}$			
$\frac{4}{25}$			

Lesson 4.7 Changing Decimals to Fractions

Decimals represent quantities such as tenths, hundredths, and thousandths. So, you can easily convert a decimal to a fraction and then simplify if needed.

$0.4 =$

$\dfrac{4}{10}$

4: 1, ②, 4
10: 1, 2, ⑤, 10

$\dfrac{4 \div 2}{10 \div 2} = \dfrac{2}{5}$

Illustrate each decimal. Then, show it as a fraction and put it in simplest form.

Decimal	Illustration	Fraction	Simplest Form
0.6			
0.35			

Lesson 4.8   Using Fractions in the Real World

Using what you have learned about fractions, solve the real-world problems below.
Show your work.

Amanda and Larry's mom made two equally sized pans of brownies. She cut one
pan into 8 equal pieces and the other pan into 9 equal pieces. Amanda ate 3
brownies from the pan cut into 8 pieces. Larry ate 4 brownies from the pan cut into
9 pieces. Who ate a larger amount of brownies: Amanda or Larry?

Shara and Maria just found out their grades for a science project. Shara received
$\frac{19}{20}$ of the possible points for the project. Maria received 0.95 of the possible points.
Who received the highest grade?

Check What You Learned

Understanding Fractions

Change the improper fraction to a mixed number. Change the mixed number to an improper fraction. Show your work.

1. $\dfrac{41}{10}$ _____

2. $5\dfrac{4}{5}$ _____

Simplify the fractions. Show your work. Explain how you know your answers cannot be simplified any more.

3. $\dfrac{15}{90}$ _____

_____

_____

4. $\dfrac{16}{52}$ _____

_____

_____

Check What You Learned

Understanding Fractions

Put these fractions in order from least to greatest. Show your work.

5. $\dfrac{3}{4}$, $\dfrac{2}{3}$, $\dfrac{5}{7}$

Convert each fraction into a decimal. Convert each decimal into a fraction. Illustrate to show your work.

6. 0.45 _____

7. $\dfrac{33}{100}$ _____

Solve the problem. Show your work.

8. Greg and Maxine want to compare how much snow has fallen at each of their houses. Greg uses a ruler to measure the snow outside his house and finds that $3\frac{1}{4}$ inches have fallen. Maxine measures using a gauge and finds that 3.29 inches have fallen at her house. Which house received more snow?

Check What You Know

Operations with Fractions

Add or subtract. Write answers in simplest form. Show your work.

1. $\dfrac{3}{8} + \dfrac{1}{8} =$

2. $4\dfrac{1}{2} + 1\dfrac{1}{3} =$

3. $3\dfrac{3}{8} - 1\dfrac{2}{3} =$

4. $\dfrac{9}{10} - \dfrac{3}{10} =$

Multiply or divide. Write answers in simplest form. Show your work.

5. $\dfrac{1}{3} \times \dfrac{4}{5} =$

6. $1\dfrac{5}{6} \times 2\dfrac{3}{4} =$

7. $\dfrac{3}{8} \div 3 =$

8. $4 \div \dfrac{1}{6} =$

Check What You Know

Operations with Fractions

Solve each problem. Show your work.

9. Sarah made fruit salad for a party. She added $2\frac{1}{2}$ cups of grapes, 4 cups of watermelon, $\frac{3}{4}$ cup of blueberries, and $3\frac{1}{3}$ cups of pineapple. She set aside $1\frac{1}{2}$ cups of fruit salad to eat. How much is left for the party?

10. Paul, Stephanie, Kayla, and Ned went on a road trip. The trip was 140 miles. Paul drove $\frac{1}{2}$ of the way, and Stephanie drove $\frac{1}{4}$ of the way. Kayla and Ned split the rest of the driving equally. How far did Ned drive?

Lesson 5.1 Adding with Like Denominators

Adding fractions with like denominators is simple because the fractions represent equal portions. For example, the fifths in the squares below are equal portions. So, the denominator does not change when the two fractions are added together.

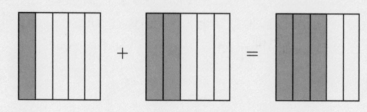

$$\frac{1}{5} + \frac{2}{5} = \frac{1+2}{5} = \frac{3}{5}$$

Use the same strategy to add mixed numbers with like denominators.

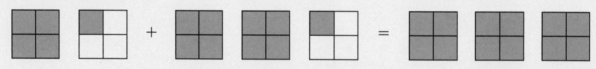

$$1\frac{1}{4} + 2\frac{1}{4} = 3\frac{1+1}{4} = 3\frac{2}{4} = 3\frac{1}{2}$$

Illustrate and add. Make sure the sum is in simplest form.

$$\frac{1}{3} + 4\frac{1}{3} = \underline{\hspace{2cm}}$$

Lesson 5.2   Subtracting with Like Denominators

Use the same approach for subtracting fractions with like denominators as you do for adding.

$$\frac{5}{6} - \frac{2}{6} = \frac{5-2}{6} = \frac{3}{6} = \frac{1}{2}$$

If regrouping is needed, use the denominator for the base.

$$4\frac{3}{8} - 1\frac{7}{8} = 3\frac{11}{8} - 1\frac{7}{8} = 2\frac{4}{8} = 2\frac{1}{2}$$

Illustrate and subtract. Make sure the difference is in simplest form.

$$9\frac{1}{5} - 3\frac{4}{5} = \underline{\hspace{2cm}}$$

Lesson 5.3 Adding with Unlike Denominators

To add fractions or mixed numbers with unlike denominators, use the least common multiple to find a denominator that represents equal portions. Then, create equivalent fractions. Finally, add the fractions or mixed numbers. If needed, convert to a mixed number or put in simplest form.

$$\frac{5}{8} + \frac{3}{4} = \frac{5}{8} + \frac{6}{8} = \frac{11}{8} = 1\frac{3}{8}$$

Add. If needed, convert the sum to a mixed number or put it in simplest form.

$4\frac{1}{2} + 2\frac{1}{3} =$

$3\frac{4}{5} + 2\frac{7}{10} =$

Lesson 5.4 Subtracting with Unlike Denominators

To subtract fractions or mixed numbers with unlike denominators, use the least common multiple to find a denominator that represents equal portions. Then, create equivalent fractions. Finally, subtract the fractions or mixed numbers. If needed, convert to a mixed number or put in simplest form.

$$3\frac{5}{6} - \frac{1}{12} = 3\frac{10}{12} - \frac{1}{12} = 3\frac{9}{12} = 3\frac{3}{4}$$

Subtract. Put the difference in simplest form.

$$5\frac{1}{2} - 3\frac{1}{3} =$$

$$7\frac{3}{8} - 2\frac{5}{6} =$$

Lesson 5.5 Multiplying with Models

When whole numbers are multiplied, the product is greater than either of the factors. When fractions are multiplied, the product is usually less than the factors.

To illustrate multiplying fractions, draw a picture showing the first factor. Then, draw a picture showing the other fraction. Lay the two drawings on top of each other to see the product.

 × 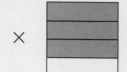 =  $\dfrac{2}{3} \times \dfrac{3}{4} = \dfrac{6}{12} = \dfrac{1}{2}$

Draw models to illustrate and solve the multiplication problems.

$\dfrac{4}{5} \times \dfrac{7}{8} =$

$1\dfrac{1}{2} \times \dfrac{4}{5} =$

Lesson 5.6 Multiplying with Rules

To multiply fractions using rules, multiply the numerators. Then, multiply the denominators. If the fractions are mixed numbers, change them into improper fractions before multiplying. Then, if needed, convert the product back into a mixed number.

$$\frac{3}{4} \times \frac{1}{8} = \frac{3 \times 1}{4 \times 8} = \frac{3}{32} \qquad 2\frac{1}{3} \times 1\frac{1}{2} = \frac{7}{3} \times \frac{3}{2} = \frac{7 \times 3}{3 \times 2} = \frac{21}{6} = 3\frac{3}{6} = 3\frac{1}{2}$$

Show how to solve each problem using a model and using the rule for multiplying fractions.

$$\frac{2}{5} \times \frac{5}{6} =$$

$$3\frac{1}{4} \times \frac{1}{2} =$$

Lesson 5.7 Dividing Unit Fractions by Whole Numbers

A unit fraction is any fraction with 1 as the numerator, such as $\frac{1}{2}$ or $\frac{1}{5}$.

When you divide a unit fraction by a whole number, the whole number splits the fraction into smaller portions. On the fraction bar below, the whole number splits each $\frac{1}{3}$ in 2 equal parts.

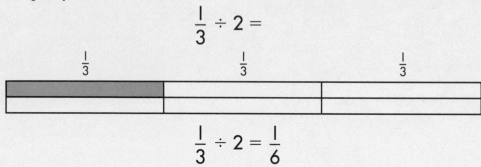

$$\frac{1}{3} \div 2 =$$

$$\frac{1}{3} \div 2 = \frac{1}{6}$$

Draw fraction bars to divide the unit fractions by whole numbers.

$$\frac{1}{4} \div 3 =$$

$$\frac{1}{2} \div 5 =$$

Lesson 5.8 Dividing Whole Numbers by Unit Fractions

To divide a whole number by a unit fraction, draw out the whole numbers first. Then, split each of them into the number given by the divisor, or unit fraction. Then, count up the total number of portions the whole numbers are split into.

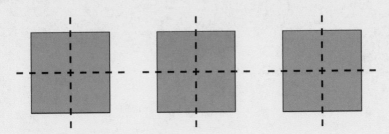

$$3 \div \frac{1}{4} = 12$$

Illustrate to find the quotient of the division problems below.

$$5 \div \frac{1}{3} =$$

$$7 \div \frac{1}{5} =$$

Lesson 5.9 Fraction Operations in the Real World

Tell which operation should be used to solve the real-world problem. Then, solve the problem using a strategy from this chapter.

Nathan ate $\frac{1}{4}$ of a box of cereal for breakfast and his sister ate $\frac{1}{6}$ of it. How much of the cereal did they eat together?

Operation to use: _____

The Smith family had pizza for dinner last night. There is $\frac{1}{8}$ of a pizza left. If Mom eats $\frac{1}{2}$ of what is left for lunch, how much of the total pizza did she eat for lunch?

Operation to use: _____

A bag of cat food contains 10 cups of food. If a cat eats $\frac{1}{4}$ of a cup each day, how long will the bag of cat food last?

Operation to use: _____

Check What You Learned

Operations with Fractions

Add or subtract. Put your answer in simplest form.

1. $\dfrac{3}{7} + \dfrac{3}{8} =$

2. $5\dfrac{1}{6} - 2\dfrac{1}{3} =$

Multiply or divide using models. Show your work.

3. $\dfrac{2}{3} \times \dfrac{7}{10} =$

4. $9 \div \dfrac{1}{3} =$

Check What You Learned

Operations with Fractions

Illustrate and divide. Put your answers in simplest form.

5. $\frac{1}{4} \div 5 =$ _____

6. $2 \div \frac{1}{8} =$ _____

Tell which operation should be used to solve the real-world problem. Then, solve the problem using rules.

7. Ronald lives $4\frac{2}{3}$ miles from school and Francis lives $2\frac{3}{5}$ miles from school. How much closer does Francis live?

Operation to use: _____

Mid-Test Chapters 1–5

Multiply using the standard method.

1. 8762
   × 64
   _____

2. 2643
   × 89
   _____

Divide using an area model.

3. 1,984 ÷ 32 = _____

Divide using long division.

4. 72)11736

5. 34)8976

Mid-Test Chapters 1–5

Follow the directions for the number.

3,<u>1</u>83

6. Write the value of the underlined digit.

   _____

7. Write the number in expanded form.

   _____

8. Round the number to the underlined digit.

   _____

9. Write the rounded number as a power of ten to the ones place.

   _____

Write the missing value.

10. $6,449,472 = 6,000,000 +$ _____ $+ 40,000 + 9,000 + 400 + 70 + 2$

11. Write these numbers in order on the number line: 3.27, 3.72, 3.072, 3.07.

3 ————————————————————————→ 4

CHAPTERS 1–5 MID-TEST

Mid-Test Chapters 1–5

Round each pair of numbers to the underlined digit. Then, compare using **<**, **>**, or **=**.

12. 3,4̲82.13; 3,49̲4.98

13. 467.3̲5; 467.47̲6

_____ ___ _____

_____ ___ _____

14. Multiply using rules: 3,729.1 × 8.75

15. Divide using models: $\frac{3.6}{12}$

Convert the improper fraction to a mixed number. Convert the mixed number to a fraction. Show your work.

16. $\frac{67}{12}$

17. $3\frac{8}{9}$

Mid-Test Chapters 1–5

Put the following fractions in order from least to greatest. Illustrate to show your work.

18. $\dfrac{2}{3}$, $\dfrac{5}{6}$, $\dfrac{3}{4}$ _____

Solve the problem. Show your work.

19. Travis started a lawn care business. He charged $7.25 per hour for mowing, $13.25 per hour for pulling weeds, and $4.50 per hour for trimming bushes. In July, Travis spent 20 hours mowing, 10 hours pulling weeds, and 3 hours trimming bushes. In August, he spent 25 hours mowing, 5 hours pulling weeds, and $4\frac{1}{2}$ hours trimming bushes. In which month did he make more money?

Check What You Know

Understanding Mathematical Equations

Complete the table for the numerical pattern, and then graph the pattern.

1.

	Add 1
1	
2	
3	
4	

2.

1	2
2	4
3	6
4	8

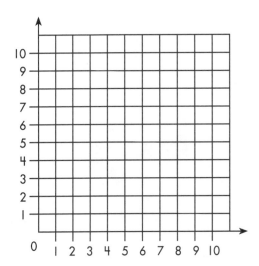

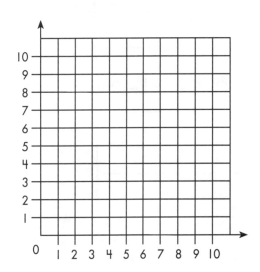

Solve the equation. Show your work.

3. $6 \div (2 + 4) + 3 =$ _____

NAME _____

Check What You Know

Understanding Mathematical Equations

Write the expressions that should be used to solve the problems below. Fill in the words that helped you figure out which operations to use.

4. 8 less than the product of 12 and 2

Key Words	Operations

_____

5. 27 divided by the difference between 13 and 4

Key Words	Operations

_____

Write the expression needed to solve the problem.

6. Jake bought 6 cases of juice boxes and 12 cases of soda. There are 8 juice boxes in one case and 6 soda cans in one case. How many more soda cans than juice boxes did Jake buy?

_____

Lesson 6.1 Generating Number Patterns

You can use rules to generate a number pattern. For the first pattern, add 1 to each number in the middle column. For the second pattern, add 2 to each number on the left.

	Add 1	Add 2
14	15	16
15	16	17
16	17	18
17	18	19

Use the rules given to generate number patterns.

	Multiply by 2	Multiply by 3
20		
25		
30		
35		

	Add 4	Add 8
16		
20		
24		
28		

	Subtract 5	Subtract 10
35		
40		
45		
50		

	Divide by 2	Divide by 3
6		
12		
18		
24		

Lesson 6.2 Identifying Number Patterns

You can examine the relationships between numbers in a pattern to find the rule used to create the pattern.

	Add 2	Add 4
12	14	16
14	16	18
16	18	20
18	20	22

Use the numbers given to find the rule used to complete the pattern. Explain your answer.

9	27	45
12	36	60
15	45	75
18	54	90

Explain: _____

_____

_____

_____

4	2	1
8	4	2
12	6	3
16	8	4

Explain: _____

_____

_____

_____

Lesson 6.3 Graphing Number Patterns

When a mathematical pattern exists, you can graph it on a coordinate grid to understand the relationship between the numbers.

	Add 3
1	4
2	5
3	6
4	7

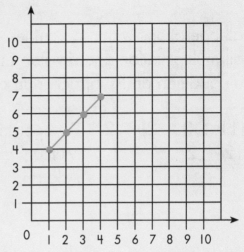

Each pair of numbers makes an ordered pair:
(1, 4), (2, 5), (3, 6), (4, 7)

Complete the pattern table below. Then, graph the pattern.

	Multiply by 2
1	
2	
3	
4	

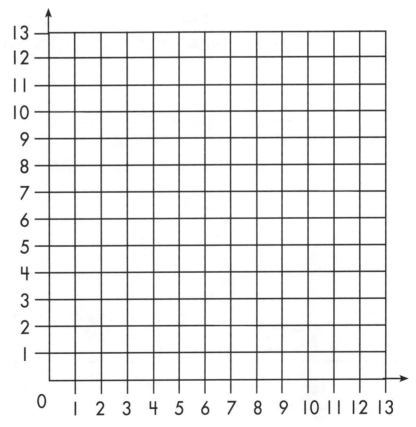

Lesson 6.4 Order of Operations

The **order of operations** is used to find the value of an expression with more than one kind of operation.

1. Do all operations within parentheses, braces, or brackets.
2. Do all multiplication and division in order, from left to right.
3. Do all addition and subtraction in order, from left to right.

$36 \div (11 + 3 - 2) + 2$	Do operations inside parentheses, braces, or brackets.
$36 \div 12 + 2$	Multiply and divide from left to right.
$3 + 2$	Add and subtract from left to right.
5	

Use complete sentences to explain the order of operations needed for each problem. Then, solve.

Kate has $300. She spends $150 on food. She spends half of what she has left on clothes. Then, she finds $24 more in a coat pocket. How much money does Kate have left?

_____

_____

Marvin bought 3 packs of pencils for $1.50 each, 2 packs of markers for $3.25 each, and 5 notebooks for $0.99 each. If Marvin started with $35, how much does he have left?

_____

_____

_____

Lesson 6.5 Simple Expressions

Key words can help you write simple expressions to solve word problems. The tables below show some key words.

Key Words	Operation
more than	addition
less than	subtraction
difference	subtraction

Key Words	Operation
times	multiplication
half	division
divided by	division

Write a simple expression for each problem. Then, solve each problem using order of operations.

Tom is 6 inches shorter than Pete, who is 8 inches taller than Jerry. If Tom is 64 inches tall, how tall is Jerry?

Expression:_____ Answer:_____

The grocery store has 4 times the number of apples as it does oranges. If the grocery store has 17 oranges, how many apples does the grocery store have?

Expression:_____ Answer:_____

Meredith scored the highest grade on the math test with a 98. Jeremy scored 6 points less than Meredith. Suzanne received half of Jeremy's score. What did Suzanne score on her test?

Expression:_____ Answer:_____

Lesson 6.6 Equations in the Real World

Review the problem structures for math operations.

Add or Subtract	Multiply or Divide
add to or take from	equal groups
put together or take apart	arrays
compare	compare

Create an equation to answer each question. Then, solve.

Ticket prices to the zoo are $10 for adults and $7 for children. Teachers get in for free. There are 130 fifth-grade students and 5 teachers. If the zoo requires 1 adult to attend for every 10 students, how many adults will need to attend in addition to the 5 teachers?

Expression: _____

Solution: _____

How much will the trip to the zoo cost?

Expression: _____

Solution: _____

Explain how you calculated the total cost of adult tickets.

_____

_____

Check What You Learned

Understanding Mathematical Equations

Complete the table for the numerical pattern. Then, graph the pattern.

1.

	Add 5
1	
2	
3	
4	

2.

3	1
6	2
9	3
12	4

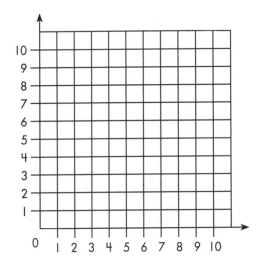

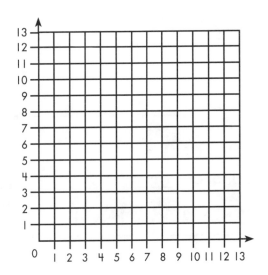

Solve the equation. Show your work. Then, list the operations you used in order.

3. $42 \div (6 + 1) \times 2 = $ _____

a) _____

b) _____

c) _____

Check What You Learned

Understanding Mathematical Equations

Create an equation to solve this real-world problem. Then, solve and explain the clues you used.

4. Olivia is playing a video game. She hits 10 bonuses that are worth 250 points each. Every time she passes a level, she gets a 500-point bonus. Her base scores are 150 on level 1, 275 on level 2, 330 on level 3, and 355 on level 4. If the high score on the video game is 7,200, how many points will she need to reach the high score when she passes level 5?

Equation: _____

Solution: _____

Explanation: _____

_____

_____

Check What You Know

Measurement

Convert the measurements below.

1. 27 feet = _____ yards

2. 1,000 centimeters = _____ meters

3. 5,600 grams = _____ centigrams

4. 80 ounces = _____ pounds

Create a line plot to show the situation. Then, solve the problem.

5. A group of friends meet at a restaurant. Fred places an order for 5 chicken wings. Mike and Tony each place an order for 8 wings. John, Jake, and Jim order 10 wings each. Al orders 12 wings. How many wings did they order in all?

Fill in the missing numbers. Then, find the perimeter and area of the shape. Show your work.

6.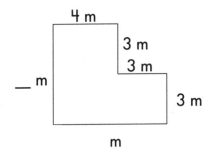

P = _____ m

A = _____ m^2

Check What You Know

Measurement

Find the volume of the figure below. Explain how you got your answer.

7.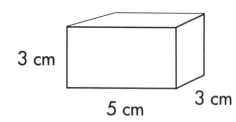

3 cm

5 cm   3 cm

V = _____

Solve the word problems. Show your work.

8. Joan needs to buy new carpet for the two bedrooms in her house. The bedrooms are 12 feet by 10 feet and 15 feet by 18 feet. How many square feet of carpet does Joan need to buy?

9. The new fish tank is 28 inches long, 12 inches high, and 16 inches deep. How many cubic inches of water will it take to fill the tank?

Lesson 7.1 Standard Measurement Conversions

Length	Volume	Weight
1 mile (mi.) = 1,760 yards (yd.)	1 gallon (gal.) = 4 quarts (qt.)	
1 mile (mi.) = 5,280 feet (ft.)	1 gallon (gal.) = 8 pints (pt.)	1 pound (lb.) = 16 ounces (oz.)
1 yard (yd.) = 36 inches (in.)	1 quart (qt.) = 2 pints (pt.)	
1 yard (yd.) = 3 feet (ft.)	1 quart (qt.) = 4 cups (c.)	2,000 pounds (lb.) = 1 ton (T.)
1 foot (ft.) = 12 inches (in.)	1 pint (pt.) = 2 cups (c.)	

Solve the measurement problems using the conversion table. Show your work.

A football field is 100 yards long. If Mike throws the football 273 feet from one end of the field, how many more yards is it to the other end of the field?

Marissa needs 1 gallon of iced tea for the cookout. She has 8 cups already. If she is making the tea in a 1-pint pitcher, how many pints does she need to make?

A truck has a capacity of 2 tons. If the truck is already loaded with 3,587 pounds of coal, how many more pounds can it hold?

Lesson 7.2   Metric Measurement Conversions

Length	Weight	Volume
1 kilometer (k) = 1,000 meters (m)	1 kilogram (kg) = 1,000 grams (g)	1 kiloliter (kL) = 1,000 liters (L)
1 meter (m) = 0.001 kilometers (km)	1 gram (g) = 0.001 kilograms (kg)	1 liter (L) = 0.001 kiloliters (kL)
1 meter (m) = 100 centimeters (cm)	1 gram (g) = 100 centigrams (cg)	1 liter (L) = 100 centiliters (cL)
1 centimeter (cm) = 0.01 meters (m)	1 centigram (cg) = 0.01 grams (g)	1 centiliter (cL) = 0.01 liters (L)
1 meter (m) = 1,000 millimeters (mm)	1 gram (g) = 1,000 milligrams (mg)	1 liter (L) = 1,000 milliliters (mL)
1 millimeter (mm) = 0.001 meter (m)	1 milligram (mg) = 0.001 gram (g)	1 milliliter (mL) = 0.001 liters (L)

Solve the measurement problems using the conversion table. Show your work.

The bulletin board for the classroom is 5 meters long. Ms. Jones has 190 centimeters of fabric to cover the board. How much more fabric is needed?

A paper clip weighs about 1 gram. If 100 paper clips come in a box, how many boxes of paper clips will be needed to make the weight of one kilogram?

The science experiment requires 4 centiliters of vinegar. If the vinegar bottle has 1.5 liters in it, how many centiliters will be left after the experiment?

Lesson 7.3 Using Line Plots to Solve Problems

A **line plot** is used to mark how many times something occurs in a data set. Line plots can help organize information to solve problems.

A pitcher holds 3 quarts of punch. There are several glasses being filled from the pitcher that hold various amounts: 3 glasses hold $\frac{1}{8}$ qt., 2 glasses hold $\frac{1}{4}$ qt., and 5 glasses hold $\frac{1}{3}$ qt. How much punch will be left in the pitcher after all the glasses are filled?

$$3 - [(3 \times \tfrac{1}{8}) + (2 \times \tfrac{1}{4}) + (5 \times \tfrac{1}{3})] =$$

$$3 - (\tfrac{3}{8} + \tfrac{2}{4} + \tfrac{5}{3}) = 3 - (\tfrac{9}{24} + \tfrac{12}{24} + \tfrac{40}{24}) =$$

$$\tfrac{72}{24} - \tfrac{61}{24} = \tfrac{11}{24} \text{ qt.}$$

```
                    x
                    x
  x                 x
  x       x         x
  x       x         x
+---+---+---+
  1       1       1
  -       -       -
  8       4       3
```

Create a line plot to answer the question. Show your work and explain your answer.

Kendra and her friends buy gummy worms at the candy store. Kendra buys $\frac{1}{3}$ pound of gummy worms. Two of her friends buy $\frac{1}{4}$ pound each, and three other friends buy $\frac{1}{2}$ pound each. The store offers a discount for buying 3 pounds or more of candy. Do Kendra and her friends qualify for the discount?

Lesson 7.4   Perimeter of Irregular Shapes

To find the perimeter of an irregular shape, find the lengths of all the sides and add them together.

$5 + 1 + 1 + 3 + 1 + 1 + 5 + 1 + 1 + 3 + 1 + 1 =$

$\qquad$ 24 inches

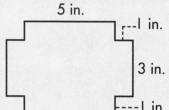

Fill in the missing numbers. Then, find the perimeter of each shape. Show your work.

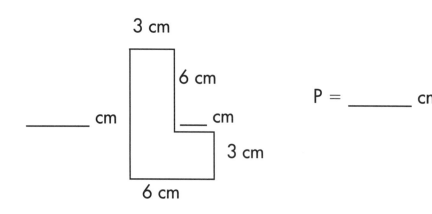

P = _____ cm

P = _____ ft.

Lesson 7.5 Area of Irregular Shapes

To find the area of an irregular polygon, decompose to create simple polygons. Then, add the area of each simple polygon together.

Polygon 1 = 8 ft. × 6 ft. = 48 square feet

Polygon 2 = 2 ft. × 2 ft. = 4 square feet

Polygon area = 48 square feet + 4 square feet

Polygon area = 52 square feet

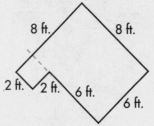

Decompose the irregular polygon to find its area. Show your work. Use lines to show how the polygon was decomposed.

A = _____ in.^{2}

4 in. 4 in. 4 in.

4 in. 4 in.

4 in. 4 in.

4 in.

Show two different ways to decompose the irregular polygon. Then, find the area both ways.

A = _____ in.^{2}

3 in.

3 in. 1 in.

2 in.

6 in. 2 in. 5 in.

6 in.

3 in.

3 in. 1 in.

2 in.

6 in. 2 in. 5 in.

6 in.

Lesson 7.6   Calculating Volume with Unit Cubes

You can find the volume of a rectangular solid by figuring out how many cubes of a particular unit size will fit inside the shape.

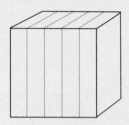

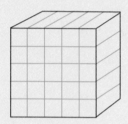

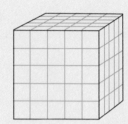

First, divide the figure into given length units.

Next, divide the figure into given height units.

Last, divide the figure into given width units.

$$5 \times 5 \times 5 = 125$$

Illustrate and multiply to find the volume of the rectangular solids.

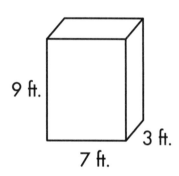

9 ft. 7 ft. 3 ft.

_____ × _____ × _____ =

_____ cubic ft.

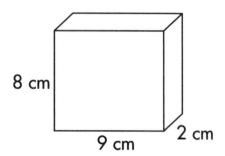

8 cm   9 cm   2 cm

_____ × _____ × _____ =

_____ cubic cm

Lesson 7.7 Calculating Volume with Multiplication

To find the volume of a rectangular solid, you can multiply the length, height, and width.

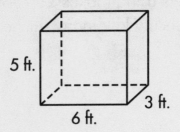

Volume = length × width × height

Volume = 6 ft. × 3 ft. × 5 ft.

Volume = 90 cubic feet

A produce shipping crate for grapefruit is 9 feet long, 7 feet tall, and 2 feet wide. What is the volume of the shipping crate?

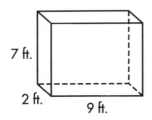

A yard waste bin is 4 feet long, 5 feet tall, and 3 feet deep. What is the volume of the yard waste bin?

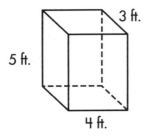

Lesson 7.8 Measurement in the Real World

Solve each problem and show your work.

Gabriel is making punch for a cookout. The recipe he is using makes 28 cups of punch. Gabriel has 1-quart pitchers for serving the punch. How many pitchers will he need?

Melissa bought a poster that is 19 inches wide and 24 inches tall. If she wants to frame the poster, how much framing material will she need?

The toy factory ships toys in crates that are 2 feet wide, 6 feet long, and 3 feet high. If each toy is 1 foot wide, 2 feet long, and 1 foot high, how many toys can go into each crate?

Check What You Learned

Measurement

Convert the measurements below. Show your work.

1. 64 cups = _____ gallons

2. 450 meters = _____ kilometers

Create a line plot to show the situation. Then, solve the problem.

3. Meg wants to try some new chocolate chip cookie recipes. The recipes call for different amounts of sugar. 2 recipes call for $\frac{1}{2}$ cup of sugar. 3 recipes call for $\frac{3}{4}$ cup of sugar. 3 recipes call for $\frac{1}{3}$ cup of sugar. How much sugar does Meg need to make all of the recipes?

Find the perimeter and area of the shape. Show your work.

4.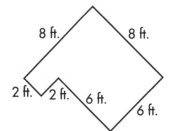

P = _____ ft.

A = _____ ft.^{2}

Check What You Learned

Measurement

Find the volume of the figure below. Show your work.

5.

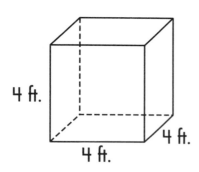

V = _____ ft.^{3}

Solve the word problems. Show your work.

6. The school wants to put a new fence around the playgrounds. One playground is 25 yards by 50 yards and the other playground is 30 yards by 45 yards. How much fencing does the school need?

7. A swimming pool is 25 meters long, 15 meters across, and 2 meters deep. How many cubic meters of water will the swimming pool hold?

Check What You Know

Geometry

Label each of the polygons and name one characteristic of that type of polygon.

1.

Name: _____

Characteristic: _____

_____

2.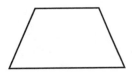

Name: _____

Characteristic: _____

_____

3.

Name: _____

Characteristic: _____

_____

4.

Name: _____

Characteristic: _____

_____

NAME _____

Check What You Know

Geometry

Plot each ordered pair on the coordinate grid.

5. A (4, 5)
   B (6, 2)
   C (1, 8)

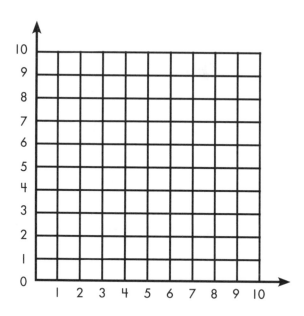

Use the coordinate grid to complete the polygon described. Answer the question and show your work.

6. A square has corners at (5, 5) and (8, 8). What are the perimeter and area of the square?

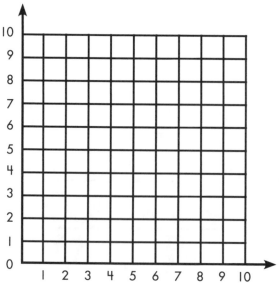

Lesson 8.1 Understanding Polygons

Every type of polygon has a unique set of characteristics. For example, a square has four equal sides and four 90-degree angles. No other polygon has those exact characteristics.

Use the word bank to fill in each blank. Then, draw the figure described.

rectangle   **trapezoid**   **equilateral triangle**

I have three equal sides and my angles add up to 180 degrees.

I am a(n) _____.

I have four right angles, two pairs of parallel sides, and two pairs of equal sides.

I am a(n) _____.

I have four sides, but only one set is parallel. My angles add up to 360 degrees.

I am a(n) _____.

Lesson 8.2 Categorizing and Classifying Polygons

Some polygons fit into more than one category. For example, a square is also a rectangle and a quadrilateral because it also fits those characteristics.

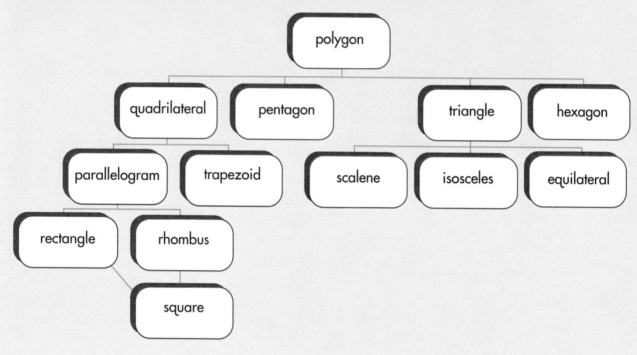

Use the chart above to complete the statements describing polygons.

All _____ are rectangles, but not all rectangles are _____.

There are _____ types of triangles: _____, _____,

and _____.

A _____ is a type of polygon, but it is not a quadrilateral.

A _____ is a type of quadrilateral that is not a parallelogram.

Lesson 8.3   Understanding Coordinate Grids

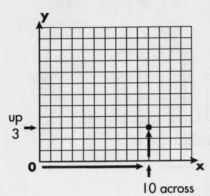

The *x-axis* runs on a horizontal line.

The *y-axis* runs on a vertical line.

x-axis

y-axis

Points located on the same grid are called **coordinate points**, or **coordinates**.

A point on a grid is located by using an **ordered pair**. An ordered pair lists the *x-axis* point first and then the *y-axis* point.

up 3

10 across

(10, 3)

(x, y)

1. Count right 10 lines.

2. From that point, go up 3.

3. Draw a point.

Draw arrows to show how to find each ordered pair. Then, mark the spot where the ordered pair is located.

(3, 7)

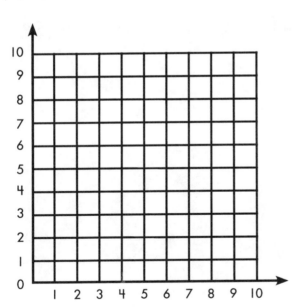

(8, 4)

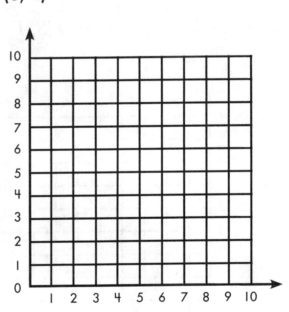

Lesson 8.4 Problem Solving with Coordinate Grids

Draw the figures described. Then, solve the problems using the coordinate grid.

A square has corners at (4, 6), (4, 9), (7, 6), and (7, 9). What is the area of the square?

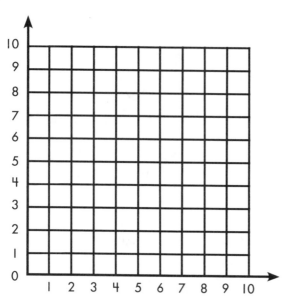

A = _____ units^2

A polygon has right angles at (3, 1), (3,7), (9,7), (9,4), (6,4), and (6,1). What is the area of the polygon?

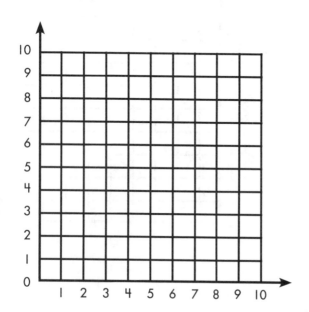

A = _____ units^2

Lesson 8.5　Geometry in the Real World

Solve the problems. Show your work.

An engineer needs to design a support for the beams on a bridge. The support must have 4 corners to distribute the weight evenly and at least one pair of parallel sides so it will be level. The top of the support cannot be wider than the base or overhang the base at any point. What shapes will work as beam supports?

Randy walks from home (2, 8) to school (7, 8) each morning. After school, he stops to meet his friend, Shane, at his house (7, 3). Then, they walk to the library (2, 3) to do their homework. After his homework is finished, Randy walks home. How far does Randy have to walk each day?

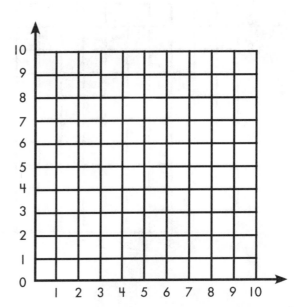

Check What You Learned

Geometry

CHAPTER 8 POSTTEST

Complete the statements about polygons.

1. A rhombus is a _____ with _____ equal sides.

2. A scalene _____ has _____ sides that are unequal.

3. A(n) _____ has 6 sides.

Draw arrows to show how to place ordered pairs on the coordinate grids.

4. (7, 4)   5. (3, 8)

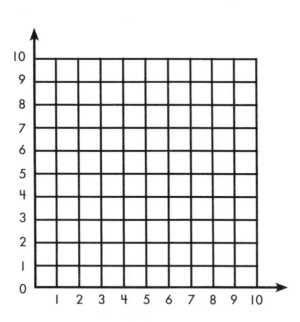   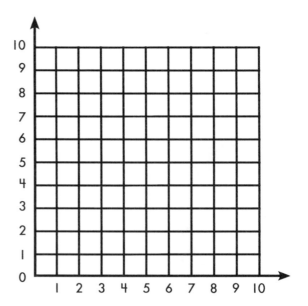

Check What You Learned

Geometry

Use the blank coordinate grid to solve the problems below.

6. A rectangle has corners at (4,3) and (6,10). What is the perimeter of the rectangle?

7. A line runs from (2,2) to (7,2). How long is the line?

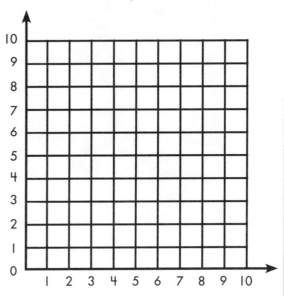

Use the blank coordinate grid to solve the problem.

8. Ginny walks from her house at (3,3) to the park at (8,3). After that, she goes to the grocery store at (8,5), the shoe store at (5,5), and the bank at (5,8). Then, she visits a friend at (3,8) before she walks back home. How far did Ginny walk today?

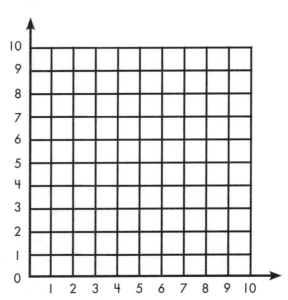

Final Test Chapters 1–8

Add, subtract, multiply, or divide using the strategy in parentheses.

1. (standard) $\begin{array}{r} 281.21 \\ \times\quad 1.2 \\ \hline \end{array}$

2. (place value) $\begin{array}{r} 8271 \\ \times\ 836 \\ \hline \end{array}$

3. (rules) $2.3\overline{)225.4}$

4. (rules) $\dfrac{3}{4} \times 2\dfrac{1}{3} =$ _____

5. (models) $8 \div \dfrac{1}{7} =$ _____

6. (rules) $\dfrac{6}{7} \times 2\dfrac{3}{14} =$ _____

Final Test Chapters 1–8

Complete the number pattern and graph it on the blank coordinate grid.

7.

	Subtract 4
6	
8	
10	
12	

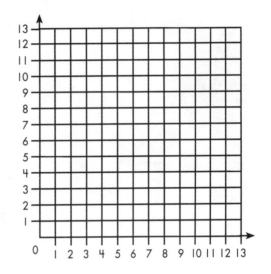

Use order of operations to solve the equations below. Show your work.

8. $13 + (9 \times 2) =$ _____

9. $(15 - 5) + 2 \times 12 =$ _____

Convert the measurements. Show your work.

10. 384 ounces = _____ pounds

11. 89 grams = _____ centigrams

Final Test Chapters 1–8

Find the area.

12.

9 cm
3 cm
3 cm
6 cm

A = _____ sq. cm

Fill in the blanks to describe polygons.

13. A square has 4 _____ sides and 4 _____ angles.

14. A trapezoid is a _____ that has _____ pair(s) of

parallel sides and _____ angles.

15. A _____ has 5 sides.

Find and label the points on the coordinate grid.

16. A at (3,7)

17. B at (4,3)

18. C at (9,10)

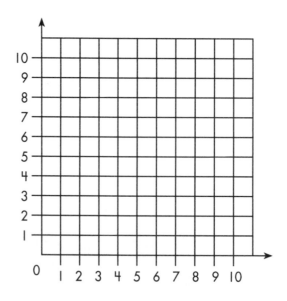

Final Test Chapters 1–8

Solve the multi-step problem below and show your work.

19. You have a vegetable garden that is 20 feet long and 13 yards and 1 foot wide. You want the dirt to be 2 feet deep. How much dirt will you need?

What is the area of the entire garden?

$\frac{1}{4}$ of the vegetable garden will be tomatoes, $\frac{1}{6}$ will be carrots, $\frac{1}{8}$ will be peppers, and $\frac{1}{4}$ will be corn. What fraction of the garden's area will those vegetables take up?

What fraction of the garden is unplanted? Draw a picture to illustrate.

Final Test   Chapters 1–8

Solve the multi-step problem below and show your work.

20. You are planning a pizza party. You have permission to invite 24 friends and you have a budget of $100. The pizza place you are ordering from will cut 14-inch pizzas into 8 slices or 12 slices. A cheese pizza costs $7.99, a 1-topping pizza costs $8.99, and a 2-topping pizza costs $10.99.

    How many pizzas of each type will you order?

How many slices will each guest be able to eat? Explain your answer. Show your work.

CHAPTERS 1–8 FINAL TEST

Spectrum Critical Thinking for Math
Grade 5

100

Chapters 1–8
Final Test

Answer Key

Page 5

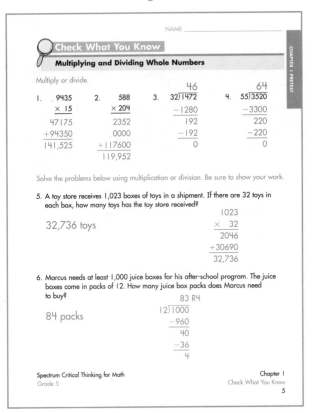

NAME _____

🔍 **Check What You Know**

Multiplying and Dividing Whole Numbers

CHAPTER 1 PRETEST

Multiply or divide.

1. 9435
    × 15
    ‾‾‾‾‾
    47175
    +94350
    ‾‾‾‾‾‾
    141,525

2. 588
    × 204
    ‾‾‾‾
    2352
    0000
    +117600
    ‾‾‾‾‾‾
    119,952

3. 46
    32)1472
    −1280
    ‾‾‾‾
    192
    −192
    ‾‾‾
    0

4. 64
    55)3520
    −3300
    ‾‾‾‾
    220
    −220
    ‾‾‾
    0

Solve the problems below using multiplication or division. Be sure to show your work.

5. A toy store receives 1,023 boxes of toys in a shipment. If there are 32 toys in each box, how many toys has the toy store received?

32,736 toys

    1023
    × 32
    ‾‾‾‾
    2046
    +30690
    ‾‾‾‾‾
    32,736

6. Marcus needs at least 1,000 juice boxes for his after-school program. The juice boxes come in packs of 12. How many juice box packs does Marcus need to buy?

84 packs

    83 R4
    12)1000
    −960
    ‾‾‾‾
    40
    −36
    ‾‾‾
    4

Spectrum Critical Thinking for Math
Grade 5

Chapter 1
Check What You Know
5

Page 6

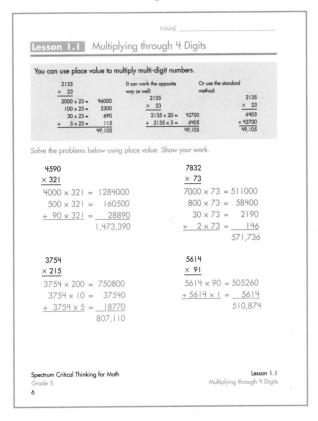

NAME _____

Lesson 1.1 Multiplying through 4 Digits

You can use place value to multiply multi-digit numbers.

2135	It can work the opposite way as well:	Or use the standard method:
× 23	2135	2135
2000 × 23 = 46000	× 23	× 23
100 × 23 = 2300	2135 × 20 = 42700	6405
30 × 23 = 690	+ 2135 × 3 = 6405	+ 42700
+ 5 × 23 = 115	49,105	49,105
49,105		

Solve the problems below using place value. Show your work.

4590
× 321
4000 × 321 = 1284000
500 × 321 = 160500
+ 90 × 321 = 28890
‾‾‾‾‾‾‾‾‾
1,473,390

7832
× 73
7000 × 73 = 511000
800 × 73 = 58400
30 × 73 = 2190
+ 2 × 73 = 146
‾‾‾‾‾‾‾‾
571,736

3754
× 215
3754 × 200 = 750800
3754 × 10 = 37540
+ 3754 × 5 = 18770
‾‾‾‾‾‾‾‾
807,110

5614
× 91
5614 × 90 = 505260
+ 5614 × 1 = 5614
‾‾‾‾‾‾‾‾
510,874

Spectrum Critical Thinking for Math
Grade 5
6

Lesson 1.1
Multiplying through 4 Digits

Page 7

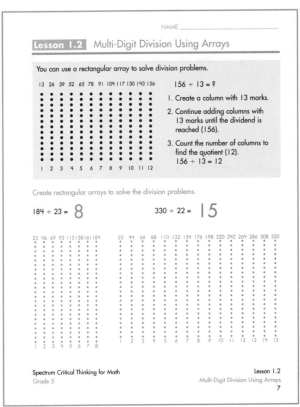

NAME _____

Lesson 1.2 Multi-Digit Division Using Arrays

You can use a rectangular array to solve division problems.

13 26 39 52 65 78 91 104 117 130 143 156

156 ÷ 13 = ?

1. Create a column with 13 marks.

2. Continue adding columns with 13 marks until the dividend is reached (156).

3. Count the number of columns to find the quotient (12).
156 ÷ 13 = 12

Create rectangular arrays to solve the division problems.

184 ÷ 23 = **8**

330 ÷ 22 = **15**

23 46 69 92 115 138 161 184

22 44 66 88 110 132 154 176 198 220 242 264 286 308 330

Spectrum Critical Thinking for Math
Grade 5

Lesson 1.2
Multi-Digit Division Using Arrays
7

Page 8

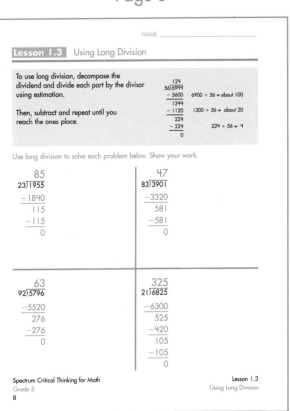

NAME _____

Lesson 1.3 Using Long Division

To use long division, decompose the dividend and divide each part by the divisor using estimation.

Then, subtract and repeat until you reach the ones place.

    124
    56)6944
    − 5600   6900 ÷ 56 = about 100
    ‾‾‾‾
    1344
    − 1120   1300 ÷ 56 = about 20
    ‾‾‾‾
    224
    − 224   224 ÷ 56 = 4
    ‾‾‾
    0

Use long division to solve each problem below. Show your work.

    85
    23)1955
    −1840
    ‾‾‾‾
    115
    −115
    ‾‾‾
    0

    47
    83)3901
    −3320
    ‾‾‾‾
    581
    −581
    ‾‾‾
    0

    63
    92)5796
    −5520
    ‾‾‾‾
    276
    −276
    ‾‾‾
    0

    325
    21)6825
    −6300
    ‾‾‾‾
    525
    −420
    ‾‾‾
    105
    −105
    ‾‾‾
    0

Spectrum Critical Thinking for Math
Grade 5
8

Lesson 1.3
Using Long Division

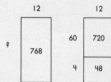

Answer Key

Page 9

NAME _____

Lesson 1.4 Using Estimation and Area Models to Divide

You can use estimation and area models to solve complicated division problems. Estimate using known multiplication and division facts.

For 768 ÷ 12, you know that 720 is close to 768, so you can use 60 × 12 as a starting point for the area model.

```
       12              12
   ┌────────┐      ┌────────┐    12 × 6 = 72, so
   │        │    60│  720   │    12 × 60 = 720
   │        │      │        │
 ? │  768   │      ├────────┤    768 − 720 = 48
   │        │     4│   48   │
   │        │      └────────┘    12 × 4 = 48
   └────────┘                    60 + 4 = 64
```

So, 768 ÷ 12 = 64

Use estimation and area models to solve these division problems. Show your work.

2,408 ÷ 43 =   4,524 ÷ 52 =
50 + 5 + 1 = 56   80 + 7 = 87

```
         43                        52
    ┌──────────┐  2408        ┌──────────┐  4524
  50│  2,150   │ −2150      80│  4,160   │ −4160
    │          │  ────        │          │  ────
    ├──────────┤   258        ├──────────┤   364
   5│   215    │ −215        7│   364    │
    ├──────────┤   ──         └──────────┘
   1│   43     │   43
    └──────────┘
```

Page 10

NAME _____

Lesson 1.5 Multiplication in the Real World

These clues tell you multiplication can be used to solve a problem.

Clue	Example
The problem describes equal groups.	There are 4 boxes with 8 games in each box. How many games are there in all?
The problem describes an array.	A rectangle is 4 inches wide and 2 inches long. What is the area of the rectangle?
The problem asks you to compare.	A bottle of water costs $2. A bottle of soda costs 2 times as much as a bottle of water. How much does a bottle of soda cost?

Solve each problem. Then, explain why each problem can be solved using multiplication.

The restaurant prepares 65 pizza crusts for every hour they are open on Saturday. If the restaurant is open for 12 hours, how many pizza crusts do they prepare?

65 x 12 = 780; equal groups of pizza crusts

An auditorium seats people in 123 rows. If there are 36 seats in each row, how many seats are in the auditorium?

123 x 36 = 4,428; an array of rows of seats

Page 11

NAME _____

Lesson 1.6 Division in the Real World

These clues tell you division can be used to solve a problem.

Clue	Example
The problem describes equal groups, and the group size or number of groups is unknown.	There are 156 cookies divided equally into 13 bags. How many cookies are in each bag?
The problem describes an array, and the number of rows or columns is unknown.	A room has an area of 225 square feet. If the room is 15 feet long, how wide is the room?
The problem asks you to compare, and the original value or multiplier is unknown.	A video game for a computer costs $10, but a game for a phone costs $2. How many times as much does the computer game cost compared to the phone game?

Solve each problem. Then, explain why each problem can be solved using division.

The school purchased 9,864 books for its fifth graders to take home over the summer. If each student takes home 12 books, how many fifth graders are in the school?

9,864 ÷ 12 = 822; equal groups of books

A combination meal with a sandwich, chips, and a drink costs $12. That price is 3 times more than 1 sandwich by itself. How much does just 1 sandwich cost?

$12 ÷ 3 = $4; it asks to compare

Page 12

NAME _____

Check What You Learned

Multiplying and Dividing Whole Numbers

Use place value to multiply. Show your work.

```
1.  8251              2.  4183
  × 64                  × 87
8000 × 64 = 512000    4000 × 87 = 348000
 200 × 64 =  12800     100 × 87 =   8700
  50 × 64 =   3200      80 × 87 =   6960
 + 1 × 64 =     64     + 3 × 87 =    261
            528,064               363,921
```

Use the standard algorithm to multiply. Show your work.

```
3.  6718        4.  4722        5.  4867
  × 19            × 48            × 39
 60462           37776           43803
+ 67180        + 188880        + 146010
127,642         226,656         189,813
```

Use long division to solve questions 6 and 7. Use estimation and area models to solve question 8.

```
        123            56                   203
6.  62)7626      7.  27)1512        8.  48)9744
    −6200            −1350              48┌──────┐   9744
    ─────            ─────               │      │  −9600
     1426             162            200 │ 9600 │   ────
    −1240            −162               │      │    144
    ─────            ────               ├──────┤   −144
      186              0              3 │ 144  │   ────
     −186                               └──────┘     0
     ────                                        200 + 3 = 203
        0
```

CHAPTER 1 POSTTEST

Answer Key

Page 13

NAME _____

💡 **Check What You Learned**

Multiplying and Dividing Whole Numbers

Solve the problems below using multiplication or division. Show your work and tell what clues helped you solve the problem.

9. A manufacturer can make 4,574 pairs of jeans in one hour. If they operate for 14 hours each day, how many pairs of jeans can they make in one day?

They can make ___64,036___ pairs of jeans.

What is the clue in this problem? ___equal groups of jeans per hour___

```
   4574
  × 14
  18296
 + 45740
  64,036
```

10. The apple orchard has 5,952 apple trees. If the trees are arranged in rows of 96, how many rows of trees are there?

There are ___62___ rows of trees.

What is the clue in this problem? _an array of trees with rows missing_

```
      62
 96)5952
   - 5760
     192
    - 192
       0
```

Spectrum Critical Thinking for Math
Grade 5

Chapter 1
Check What You Learned
13

Page 14

CHAPTER 2 PRETEST

💡 **Check What You Know**

Understanding Place Value

Follow the directions for the number.

595,682

1. Write the number in expanded form.

___500,000 + 90,000 + 5,000 + 600 + 80 + 2___

2. Divide the number by 1,000. Give your answer as a decimal.

___595.682___

3. Compare: 592,682 ___>___ 591,683

4. Write the place value of the underlined digit.

___thousands___

5. Round the number to the place value of the underlined digit.

___596,000___

6. Write the rounded number as a power of 10 to the nearest one.

___5.6×10^5___

Spectrum Critical Thinking for Math
Grade 5
14

Chapter 2
Check What You Know

Page 15

CHAPTER 2 PRETEST

💡 **Check What You Know**

Understanding Place Value

Follow the directions for the number.

58.927

7. Write the place value of the underlined digit.

___hundredths___

8. Round the number to the place value of the underlined digit.

___58.93___

9. Multiply the number by 100.

___5,892.7___

10. Compare: 58.927 ___<___ 58.94

Order the numbers from least to greatest.

11. 65.48, 6.548, 65.408, 65.485

___6.548, 65.408, 65.48, 65.485___

Spectrum Critical Thinking for Math
Grade 5

Chapter 2
Check What You Know
15

Page 16

Lesson 2.1 Identifying Place Value to Millions

Every digit in a number has a value based on its place in the number. For example, in the number 5,239,168, the 9 has a value of 9,000 because it is in the thousands place. A place value table can help you find the value.

millions	hundred thousands	ten thousands	thousands	hundreds	tens	ones
5	2	3	9	1	6	8

Use the place value table to find the value of each underlined digit. Put the values in order on the line below.

7,4<u>8</u>3,312

Value: __80,000__

4,329,6<u>7</u>3

Value: ___70___

5,9<u>4</u>2,691

Value: __2,000__

<u>8</u>,759,267

Value: __8,000,000__

___70, 2,000, 80,000, 8,000,000___

Spectrum Critical Thinking for Math
Grade 5
16

Lesson 2.1
Identifying Place Value to Millions

Answer Key

Page 17

NAME _____

Lesson 2.2 Identifying Place Value to Thousandths

In the number 4,973.562, the 6 has a value of 6 hundredths, or 0.06, because it is in the hundredths place. A place value table can help you find the value.

thousands	hundreds	tens	ones	tenths	hundredths	thousandths
4	9	7	3.	5	6	2

Tell the value of each underlined digit by using the place value table. Put the values in order on the line below.

5,689.547

Value: 0.5

9,489.392

Value: 80

6,289.365

Value: 0.06

4,392.732

Value: 0.002

0.002, 0.06, 0.5, 80

Page 18

NAME _____

Lesson 2.3 Powers of Ten

An **exponent** is a number that shows how many times a base number should be used in multiplication. It also shows how many zeros are in the number. A power of ten is created using exponents. The base number is always 10. Other numbers can also be created using powers of ten.

$$10^1 = 10 = 10$$
$$10^2 = 10 \times 10 = 100$$
$$10^3 = 10 \times 10 \times 10 = 1,000$$
$$10^4 = 10 \times 10 \times 10 \times 10 = 10,000$$

$$7 \times 10^1 = 70$$
$$7 \times 10^2 = 700$$
$$7 \times 10^3 = 7,000$$
$$7 \times 10^4 = 70,000$$

Rewrite each number as a power of ten.

90,000

9×10^4

60,000,000

6×10^7

3,000

3×10^3

Write each power of ten as a number. Compare using >, <, or =.

7×10^4

70,000

$<$

7×10^5

700,000

25×10^5

2,500,000

$<$

26×10^5

2,600,000

Page 19

NAME _____

Lesson 2.4 Expanded Form

A number written in **expanded form** shows the sum of the values of each digit. The number is separated into each of its parts using place value. This is also called **decomposing** a number.

$$3,268 = 3,000 + 200 + 60 + 8$$

$$67,491 = 60,000 + 7,000 + 400 + 90 + 1$$

Find the missing value in each expanded-form number.

$$695 = 600 + \underline{90} + 5$$

$$\underline{5,836} = 5,000 + 800 + 30 + 6$$

$$20,376 = \underline{20,000} + 300 + 70 + 6$$

$$500,913 = 500,000 + 900 + 10 + \underline{3}$$

$$\underline{954,257} = 900,000 + 50,000 + 4,000 + 200 + 50 + 7$$

Page 20

NAME _____

Lesson 2.5 Comparing and Ordering Decimals

You can compare and order decimal numbers by aligning the decimal point in each value. Then, evaluate each number in comparison with the others.

4.05 ⟶ This value is least. It has a lower value in both decimal places.
4.56 ⟶ This value is second least. It is 0.001 less than 4.561.
4.561 ⟶ This value is second greatest. It is 0.001 more than 4.56.
5.32 ⟶ This value is greatest. It has the greatest value in the ones place.

Place the values below in order from least to greatest. Explain your thinking.

7.82, 8.73, 7.802, 8.729

7.802 ⟶ Hundredths place is a 0 .

7.82 ⟶ Hundredths place is a 2 .

8.729 ⟶ Ones place is an 8. Hundredths place is a 2 .

8.73 ⟶ Ones place is an 8. Hundredths place is a 3 .

5.67, 5.607, 5.671, 5.617

5.607 ⟶ Hundredths place is a 0 .

5.617 ⟶ Hundredths place is a 1 .

5.67 ⟶ Hundredths place is a 7 .

5.671 ⟶ Hundredths place is a 7. Thousandths place is a 1 .

Page 21

NAME _____

Lesson 2.5 Rounding Whole Numbers

You can use place value to round whole numbers.

Round 51,927 to the nearest thousand.	Round 324,963 to the nearest ten.
Look at the hundreds digit: 51,<u>9</u>27	Look at the ones digit: 324,96<u>3</u>
9 is greater than or equal to 5, so round 1 to 2 in the thousands place.	3 is less than 5, so leave 6 the same in the tens place.
52,000	324,960

Round each number to the underlined place. Explain your work.

89,<u>3</u>46   89,300

___4___ is _less than_ 5, so _the 3 remains the same_ .

1<u>1</u>5,332   120,000

___5___ is _equal to_ 5, so _the 1 rounds up to 2_ .

<u>2</u>18,416   200,000

___1___ is _less than_ 5, so _the 2 remains the same_ .

Spectrum Critical Thinking for Math
Grade 5

Lesson 2.5
Rounding Whole Numbers
21

Page 22

NAME _____

Lesson 2.6 Rounding Decimals

You can use place value to round numbers with decimals.

Round 3.541 to the nearest hundredth.	Round 7.663 to the nearest tenth.
Look at the thousandths digit: 3.54<u>1</u>	Look at the hundredths digit: 7.6<u>6</u>3
1 is less than 5, so leave 4 the same in the hundredths place.	6 is greater than or equal to 5, so round 6 to 7 in the tenths place.
3.54	7.7

Round each number to the underlined place. Explain your work.

5.8<u>4</u>1   5.84

___1___ is _less than_ 5, so _the 4 remains the same_ .

2<u>9</u>.678   30

___6___ is _greater than_ 5, so _the 9 rounds up to 10_ .

6.<u>5</u>26   6.5

___2___ is _less than_ 5, so _the 5 remains the same_ .

Spectrum Critical Thinking for Math
Grade 5
22

Lesson 2.6
Rounding Decimals

Page 23

NAME _____

Lesson 2.7 Place Value in Other Systems

Time has a place value system with a base of 60.

1 hour = 60 minutes   1 minute = 60 seconds

To add or subtract, line the times up based on their place value. Use 60 as the base if regrouping is necessary.

1 hour 10 minutes + 2 hours 27 minutes	4 75 5̶ minutes 1̶5 seconds − 1 minute 30 seconds
3 hours 37 minutes	3 minutes 45 seconds

Add or subtract. Show your work.

4 min. 24 sec.
+ 2 min. 57 sec.

| 4 min. 24 sec.
+ 2 min. 57 sec.
6 min. 8̶1 sec.
+ 1   − 60
7 min. 21 sec. |

3 hr. 15 min.
− 2 hr. 20 min.

| 2   75
3̶ hr. 1̶5 min.
− 2 hr. 20 min.
55 min. |

Show how to add 1 hour 12 minutes and 10 seconds to 3 hours 4 minutes and 52 seconds using a time-based place value system.

1 hr. 12 min. 10 sec.
+ 3 hr. 4 min. 52 sec.
4 hr. 16 min. 62 sec.
____ + 1   − 60
4 hr. 17 min. 2 sec.

Spectrum Critical Thinking for Math
Grade 5

Lesson 2.7
Place Value in Other Systems
23

Page 24

NAME _____

Check What You Learned

Understanding Place Value

Find the value of each underlined digit.

1. 9,4<u>2</u>4,201   4,000

2. 4,<u>2</u>88,482   200

Write each power of ten as a number. Use <, >, or = to compare.

3. 34×10^3 35×10^2

   34,000   >   3,500

4. On the line below, put the four numbers you wrote in questions #1–4 in order from least to greatest.

   2,000   3,500   4,000   34,000

Rewrite each number as a power of ten to the ones place.

5. 9,700 9.7×10^3

6. 3,000,000 3×10^6

Find which value is incorrect in each expanded-form number.

7. 23,845 = 2,000 + 3,000 + 800 + 40 + 5   2,000 should be 20,000

8. 3,840,764 = 3,000,000 + 800,000 + 4,000 + 700 + 60 + 4
   4,000 should be 40,000

CHAPTER 2 POSTTEST

Spectrum Critical Thinking for Math
Grade 5
24

Chapter 2
Check What You Learned

Page 25

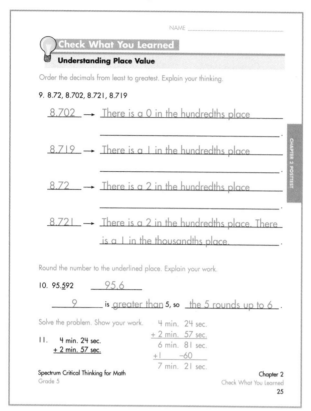

NAME _____

Check What You Learned

Understanding Place Value

Order the decimals from least to greatest. Explain your thinking.

9. 8.72, 8.702, 8.721, 8.719

__8.702__ → There is a 0 in the hundredths place
_____ .

__8.719__ → There is a 1 in the hundredths place
_____ .

__8.72__ → There is a 2 in the hundredths place
_____ .

__8.721__ → There is a 2 in the hundredths place. There
is a 1 in the thousandths place.

Round the number to the underlined place. Explain your work.

10. 95.592   __95.6__

____9____ is _greater than_ 5, so _the 5 rounds up to 6_ .

Solve the problem. Show your work.

11.   4 min. 24 sec.
    + 2 min. 57 sec.

4 min. 24 sec.
+ 2 min. 57 sec.
6 min. 81 sec.
+1   −60
7 min. 21 sec.

Spectrum Critical Thinking for Math
Grade 5

Chapter 2
Check What You Learned
25

Page 26

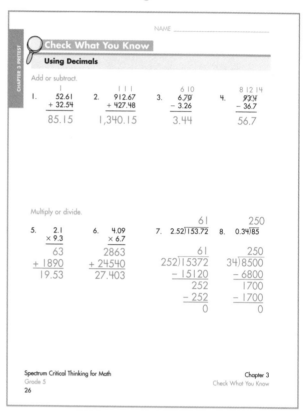

NAME _____

Check What You Know

Using Decimals

Add or subtract.

1.   1
     52.61
   + 32.54
   ─────────
    85.15

2.   1 1 1
    912.67
  + 427.48
  ─────────
  1,340.15

3.   6 10
    6.70
  − 3.26
  ─────────
    3.44

4.   8 12 14
     93.4
   − 36.7
  ─────────
    56.7

Multiply or divide.

5.   2.1
     × 9.3
   ─────────
      63
  + 1890
  ─────────
   19.53

6.   4.09
     × 6.7
   ─────────
     2863
  + 24540
  ─────────
   27.403

7. 2.52)153.72

      61
252)15372
   − 15120
      252
    − 252
        0

8. 0.34)85

      250
 34)8500
  − 6800
    1700
  − 1700
       0

Spectrum Critical Thinking for Math
Grade 5
26

Chapter 3
Check What You Know

Page 27

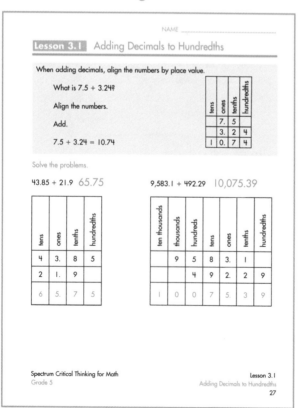

NAME _____

Lesson 3.1   Adding Decimals to Hundredths

When adding decimals, align the numbers by place value.

What is 7.5 + 3.24?

Align the numbers.

Add.

7.5 + 3.24 = 10.74

tens	ones	tenths	hundredths
	7.	5	
	3.	2	4
1	0.	7	4

Solve the problems.

43.85 + 21.9 __65.75__

tens	ones	tenths	hundredths
4	3.	8	5
2	1.	9	
6	5.	7	5

9,583.1 + 492.29 __10,075.39__

ten thousands	thousands	hundreds	tens	ones	tenths	hundredths
	9	5	8	3.	1	
		4	9	2.	2	9
1	0	0	7	5.	3	9

Spectrum Critical Thinking for Math
Grade 5

Lesson 3.1
Adding Decimals to Hundredths
27

Page 28

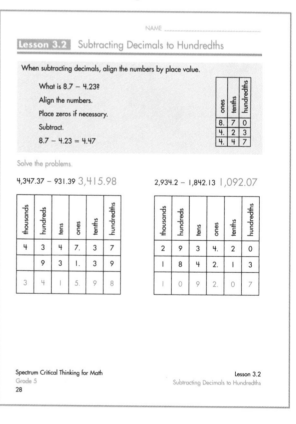

NAME _____

Lesson 3.2   Subtracting Decimals to Hundredths

When subtracting decimals, align the numbers by place value.

What is 8.7 − 4.23?

Align the numbers.

Place zeros if necessary.

Subtract.

8.7 − 4.23 = 4.47

ones	tenths	hundredths
8.	7	0
4.	2	3
4.	4	7

Solve the problems.

4,347.37 − 931.39 __3,415.98__

thousands	hundreds	tens	ones	tenths	hundredths
4	3	4	7.	3	7
	9	3	1.	3	9
3	4	1	5.	9	8

2,934.2 − 1,842.13 __1,092.07__

thousands	hundreds	tens	ones	tenths	hundredths
2	9	3	4.	2	0
1	8	4	2.	1	3
1	0	9	2.	0	7

Spectrum Critical Thinking for Math
Grade 5

Lesson 3.2
Subtracting Decimals to Hundredths
28

Answer Key

Page 29

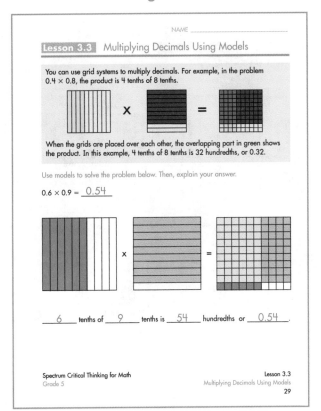

Page 30

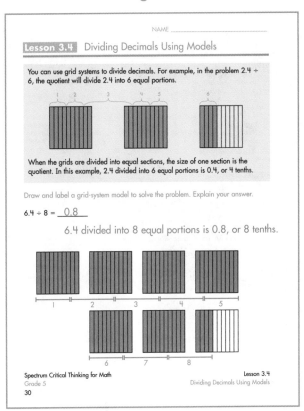

Page 31

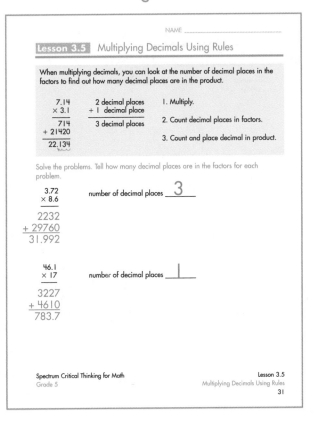

Page 32

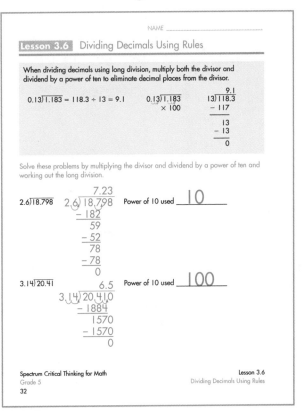

Page 33

NAME _____

Lesson 3.7 Using Decimals in the Real World

Use what you have learned about decimals to solve these multi-step problems. Show your work and tell which operations you used.

If Pete were 13.5 inches taller, he would be twice as tall as Jonathan. If Jonathan is 45.8 inches tall, how tall is Pete?

Pete is 78.1 inches tall.

$$\begin{array}{r} 45.8 \\ \times\ \ 2 \\ \hline 91.6 \end{array} \qquad \begin{array}{r} 91.6 \\ -\ 13.5 \\ \hline 78.1 \end{array}$$

Which operations did you use? First, I __multiplied__ . Then, I __subtracted__ .

Tia bought her dad a new tie for $19.95. Then, she bought her sister a new pair of earrings for $9.38. If she started with $55.00, how much money does she have left?

Tia has $25.67 left.

$$\begin{array}{r} \$19.95 \\ +\ \ 9.38 \\ \hline \$29.33 \end{array} \qquad \begin{array}{r} \$55.00 \\ -\ 29.33 \\ \hline \$25.67 \end{array}$$

Which operations did you use? First, I __added__ . Then, I __subtracted__ .

Page 34

NAME _____

Check What You Learned

Using Decimals

Add or subtract.

1. 4,323.67 + 518.9 4,842.57

thousands	hundreds	tens	ones	tenths	hundredths
4	3	2	3.	6	7
	5	1	8.	9	0
4	8	4	2.	5	7

2. 8,583.43 − 276.94 8,306.49

thousands	hundreds	tens	ones	tenths	hundredths
8	5	8	3.	4	3
	2	7	6.	9	4
8	3	0	6.	4	9

Use models to solve the problem below. Then, explain your answer.

3. 0.4 × 0.7 = __0.28__

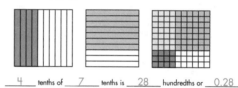

__4__ tenths of __7__ tenths is __28__ hundredths or __0.28__ .

Page 35

NAME _____

Check What You Learned

Using Decimals

Multiply or divide using rules.

4. $$\begin{array}{r} 8.56 \\ \times\ 3.72 \end{array}$$

$$\begin{array}{r} 8.56 \\ \times\ 3.72 \\ \hline 1712 \\ 59920 \\ +\ 256800 \\ \hline 31.8432 \end{array}$$

5. 2.52)153.72

$$\begin{array}{r} 61 \\ 2.52)15372 \\ -1512 \\ \hline 252 \\ -252 \\ \hline 0 \end{array}$$

Solve this multi-step decimal problem. Show your work and explain which operations you used to find your answer.

6. Michael and Michelle are twins. For their birthday, they receive $25.00 from their aunt, $32.55 from their grandmother, and $15.87 from their parents. If the twins split the money evenly, how much money will they each receive?

Each twin will receive $36.71.

$$\begin{array}{r} \$25.00 \\ 32.55 \\ +\ 15.87 \\ \hline \$73.42 \end{array}$$

$$\begin{array}{r} \$36.71 \\ 2)73.42 \\ -6 \\ \hline 13 \\ -12 \\ \hline 14 \\ -14 \\ \hline 02 \\ -2 \\ \hline 0 \end{array}$$

Which operations did you use? First, I __added__ .

Then, I __divided__ .

Page 36

NAME _____

Check What You Know

Understanding Fractions

Change improper fractions to mixed numbers and mixed numbers to improper fractions. Show your work.

1. $6\frac{1}{8}$ $\frac{49}{8}$

$6 \times 8 + 1 = 49$

2. $\frac{53}{6}$ $8\frac{5}{6}$

$53 \div 6 = 8\ R5$

Find the greatest common factor. Show your work.

3. 6, 9, 18 6: 1, 2, ③ 6; 9: 1 ③ 9; 18: 1, 2 ③ 6, 9, 18;

3 is the greatest common factor.

Find the least common multiple. Show your work.

4. 4, 5, 10 4: 4, 8, 12, 16, ⑳ 5: 5, 10, 15, ⑳ 10: 10, ⑳

20 is the least common multiple.

5. Put the fraction $\frac{12}{36}$ in simplest form.

$\frac{12 \div 12}{36 \div 12} = \frac{1}{3}$

12: 1, 2, 3, 4, 6, ⑫

36: 1, 2, 3, 4, 6, 9, ⑫ 18, 36

Answer Key

Page 37

🔍 **Check What You Know**

Understanding Fractions

Put these fractions in order from least to greatest. Draw a picture to show your work.

6. $\frac{1}{3}$, $\frac{1}{2}$, $\frac{1}{4}$

$\frac{1}{4}$, $\frac{1}{3}$, $\frac{1}{2}$

$\frac{1}{4}$ ⊕ $\frac{1}{3}$ ⊕ $\frac{1}{2}$ ◐

Convert each fraction into a decimal. Convert each decimal into a fraction. Show your work.

7. $\frac{7}{8}$

$\begin{array}{r} 0.875 \\ 8)\overline{7.000} \\ -6\,4 \\ \hline 60 \\ -56 \\ \hline 40 \end{array}$

8. 1.75

$1\frac{75 \div 25}{100 \div 25} = 1\frac{3}{4}$

75: 1, 3, 5, 15, (25) 75;
100: 1, 2, 4, 5, 10, 20, (25) 50, 100

Solve the problem. Draw a picture to show your work.

9. Lou and David order 2 pizzas of the same size for dinner. The pepperoni pizza is sliced into 8 equal pieces, and the cheese pizza is sliced into 12 equal pieces. If Lou eats 5 pieces of pepperoni pizza and David eats 7 pieces of cheese pizza, who has eaten more pizza?

Lou has eaten more pizza because $\frac{5}{8}$ is greater than $\frac{7}{12}$.

pepperoni   cheese   8 : 8, 16, (24)
⊛   ⊛   12 : 12, (24)

$\frac{5}{8} = \frac{15}{24}$ $\frac{7}{12} = \frac{14}{24}$

Page 38

Lesson 4.1 Converting Fractions

You can use multiplication and addition to convert mixed numbers to improper fractions.

$3\frac{1}{4}$ = = $\frac{13}{4}$

$3 \times 4 + 1 = 13$

You can use division and remainders to convert improper fractions to mixed numbers.

$\frac{8}{5}$ = = $1\frac{3}{5}$

$8 \div 5 = 1$ R3

Convert the mixed number to an improper fraction. Convert the improper fraction to a mixed number. Explain how each change was made.

$2\frac{2}{3}$ $\frac{8}{3}$

First, multiply the whole number by the denominator to get 6

portions. Then, add 2 to get the numerator for the improper fraction.

$\frac{9}{4}$ $2\frac{1}{4}$

First, divide 9 by 4. The quotient is the whole number, and the

remainder becomes the numerator for the fraction in the mixed number.

Page 39

Lesson 4.2 Number Relationships

When working with fractions, you will often need to find the least common multiple (LCM) and the greatest common factor (GCF) of a set of numbers.

Least Common Multiple	**Greatest Common Factor**
What is the smallest common number that is a multiple of each number?	What is the highest number that divides exactly into each number?
2: 2, 4, 6, 8, 10, (12) 3: 3, 6, 9, (12) 4: 4, 8, (12)	12: 1, 2, 3, (4) 6, 12 20: 1, 2, (4) 5, 10, 20 32: 1, 2, (4) 8, 16, 32
12 is the LCM. It is the smallest multiple found in all 3 lists.	4 is the GCF. It is the greatest factor found in all 3 lists.

Find the least common multiple by listing multiples.

5: 5, 10, 15, 20, 25, 30, 35, 40, 45, 50, 55, (60)

15: 15, 30, 45, (60)   LCM is __60__.

20: 20, 40, (60)

Find the greatest common factor by listing factors.

9: 1 (3) 9

18: 1, 2 (3) 6, 9, 18   GCF is __3__.

12: 1, 2 (3) 4, 6, 12

Page 40

Lesson 4.3 Finding Equivalent Fractions

You can use pictures, multiplication, or division to find equivalent fractions. For example, here is how to find equivalent fractions for $\frac{1}{4}$.

◔ = $\frac{1}{4}$ = ⊛ = $\frac{2}{8}$ = ⊛ = $\frac{3}{12}$

$\frac{1}{4} \begin{array}{l} \times 2 \\ \times 2 \end{array} = \frac{2}{8}$ or $\frac{3}{12} \begin{array}{l} \div 3 \\ \div 3 \end{array} = \frac{1}{4}$

List 2 fractions that are equivalent to each fraction shown. Prove the fractions are equivalent using pictures.

Fraction	Equal Fractions		Proof
$\frac{2}{3}$	$\frac{4}{6}$	$\frac{8}{12}$	⊛ ⊛ ⊛
$\frac{3}{5}$	$\frac{6}{10}$	$\frac{9}{15}$	▦ ▦ ▦

Answer Key

Page 41

NAME _____

Lesson 4.4 Simplifying Fractions

To simplify a fraction, find the greatest common factor of the numerator and denominator.

$$\frac{4}{12} \quad 4: 1, 2, ④$$
$$12: 1, 2, 3, 4, ⑥, 12$$
$$\frac{4}{12} \div 4 = \frac{1}{3}$$

Find the greatest common factor of the numerator and denominator to simplify these fractions.

$$\frac{6}{30} \qquad 6: 1, 2, 3 ⑥$$
$$\frac{6}{30} \div 6 = \frac{1}{5} \qquad 30: 1, 2, 3, 5 ⑥ 10, 15, 30$$

$$\frac{8}{24} \qquad 8: 1, 2, 4 ⑧$$
$$\frac{8}{24} \div 8 = \frac{1}{3} \qquad 24: 1, 2, 3, 4, 6 ⑧ 12, 24$$

$$\frac{15}{35} \qquad 15: 1, 3 ⑤ 15$$
$$\frac{15}{35} \div 5 = \frac{3}{7} \qquad 35: 1 ⑤ 7, 35$$

Spectrum Critical Thinking for Math
Grade 5

Lesson 4.4
Simplifying Fractions
41

Page 42

NAME _____

Lesson 4.5 Comparing and Ordering Fractions

The denominator is a clue about the size of the fraction. If the denominator is larger, the portion that one part of the fraction represents will be smaller.

 $\frac{1}{4}$ is greater than $\frac{1}{8}$

You can put fractions in order when they have different numerators and denominators. Find the least common multiple of the denominators so the fractions represent equal portions. Then, compare the numerators.

$$\frac{2}{5} \qquad \frac{1}{3} \qquad \frac{5}{6}$$

$$\frac{2}{5} = \frac{12}{30} \qquad \frac{1}{3} = \frac{10}{30} \qquad \frac{5}{6} = \frac{25}{30}$$

$$\frac{10}{30} < \frac{12}{30} < \frac{25}{30} = \frac{1}{3} < \frac{2}{5} < \frac{5}{6}$$

Put the fractions in order from least to greatest. Find the least common multiple of the denominators to tell how many portions you need to compare the fractions.

$$\frac{1}{4}, \frac{2}{5}, \frac{3}{10} \qquad \frac{1}{4}, \frac{3}{10}, \frac{2}{5}$$

4: 4, 8, 12, 16, ⑳

5: 5, 10, 15, ⑳

10: 10, ⑳

LCM is 20.

$$\frac{1}{4} = \frac{5}{20}$$
$$\frac{2}{5} = \frac{8}{20}$$
$$\frac{3}{10} = \frac{6}{20}$$

Spectrum Critical Thinking for Math
Grade 5

Lesson 4.5
Comparing and Ordering Fractions
42

Page 43

NAME _____

Lesson 4.6 Changing Fractions to Decimals

You can change fractions into decimals using mathematical operations.

$$\frac{1}{4}$$

$$1 \div 4 = 4\overline{)1.00} = 0.25$$
$$\frac{0.25}{}$$
$$-8$$
$$\overline{20}$$
$$-20$$
$$\overline{0}$$

Use division to change these fractions into decimals. Illustrate using the grids.

Fraction	Illustration	Divide	Decimal
$\frac{3}{10}$		$10\overline{)3.0}$ $\frac{0.3}{}$ -30 $\overline{0}$	0.3
$\frac{4}{25}$		$25\overline{)4.00}$ $\frac{0.16}{}$ -25 $\overline{150}$ -150 $\overline{0}$	0.16

Spectrum Critical Thinking for Math
Grade 5

Lesson 4.6
Changing Fractions to Decimals
43

Page 44

NAME _____

Lesson 4.7 Changing Decimals to Fractions

Decimals represent quantities such as tenths, hundredths, and thousandths. So, you can easily convert a decimal to a fraction and then simplify if needed.

$$0.4 = \qquad \frac{4}{10} \quad 4: 1, ② 4 \qquad \frac{4}{10} \div 2 = \frac{2}{5}$$
$$10: 1, 2 ⑤ 10$$

Illustrate each decimal. Then, show it as a fraction and put it in simplest form.

Decimal	Illustration	Fraction	Simplest Form
0.6		$\frac{6}{10}$	$\frac{3}{5}$
0.35		$\frac{35}{100}$	$\frac{7}{20}$

Spectrum Critical Thinking for Math
Grade 5

Lesson 4.7
Changing Decimals to Fractions
44

Answer Key

Page 45

NAME _____

Lesson 4.8 Using Fractions in the Real World

Using what you have learned about fractions, solve the real-world problems below. Show your work.

Amanda and Larry's mom made two equally sized pans of brownies. She cut one pan into 8 equal pieces and the other pan into 9 equal pieces. Amanda ate 3 brownies from the pan cut into 8 pieces. Larry ate 4 brownies from the pan cut into 9 pieces. Who ate a larger amount of brownies: Amanda or Larry?

8: 8, 16, 24, 32, 40, 48, 56, 64, (72) $\frac{3}{8} = \frac{27}{72}$

9: 9, 18, 27, 36, 45, 54, 63, (72) $\frac{4}{9} = \frac{32}{72}$

$\frac{27}{72} < \frac{32}{72}$

If you compare the fractions with a common denominator, $\frac{4}{9}$ is more than $\frac{3}{8}$. So, Larry ate a larger amount.

Shara and Maria just found out their grades for a science project. Shara received $\frac{19}{20}$ of the possible points for the project. Maria received 0.95 of the possible points. Who received the highest grade?

$\frac{19}{20} = 19 \div 20$

$$\begin{array}{r} 0.95 \\ 20\overline{)19.00} \\ -180 \\ \hline 100 \\ -100 \\ \hline 0 \end{array}$$ = 0.95

If you convert $\frac{19}{20}$ to a decimal, it is 0.95. So, Shara and Maria got the same grade on the project.

Spectrum Critical Thinking for Math
Grade 5

Lesson 4.8
Using Fractions in the Real World
45

Page 46

NAME _____

💡 **Check What You Learned**

Understanding Fractions

Change the improper fraction to a mixed number. Change the mixed number to an improper fraction. Show your work.

1. $\frac{41}{10}$ $4\frac{1}{10}$ $41 \div 10 = 4 R1$

2. $5\frac{4}{5}$ $\frac{29}{5}$ $5 \times 5 + 4 = 29$

Simplify the fractions. Show your work. Explain how you know your answers cannot be simplified any more.

3. $\frac{15}{90}$ $\frac{1}{6}$ 15: 1, 3, 5, (15)
90: 1, 2, 3, 5, 6, 9, 10, (15) 18, 30, 45, 90
$\frac{15 \div 15}{90 \div 15} = \frac{1}{6}$

It cannot be reduced any more because both the numerator and denominator have been divided by the greatest common factor, 15.

4. $\frac{16}{52}$ $\frac{4}{13}$ 16: 1, 2, (4,) 8, 16
52: 1, 2, (4,) 13, 26, 52
$\frac{16 \div 4}{52 \div 4} = \frac{4}{13}$

It cannot be reduced any more because both the numerator and denominator have been divided by the greatest common factor, 4.

Spectrum Critical Thinking for Math
Grade 5
46

Chapter 4
Check What You Learned

Page 47

NAME _____

💡 **Check What You Learned**

Understanding Fractions

Put these fractions in order from least to greatest. Show your work.

5. $\frac{3}{4}, \frac{2}{3}, \frac{5}{7}$ $\frac{2}{3} < \frac{5}{7} < \frac{3}{4}$ $\frac{56}{84} < \frac{60}{84} < \frac{63}{84}$

84 portions are needed to compare these fractions because that is the least common multiple of 3, 4, and 7.

$\frac{3}{4} = \frac{63}{84}$
$\frac{2}{3} = \frac{56}{84}$ $\frac{5}{7} = \frac{60}{84}$

Convert each fraction into a decimal. Convert each decimal into a fraction. Illustrate to show your work.

6. 0.45 $\frac{9}{20}$

7. $\frac{33}{100}$ 0.33

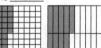

Solve the problem. Show your work.

8. Greg and Maxine want to compare how much snow has fallen at each of their houses. Greg uses a ruler to measure the snow outside his house and finds that $3\frac{1}{4}$ inches have fallen. Maxine measures using a gauge and finds that 3.29 inches have fallen at her house. Which house received more snow?

$3\frac{1}{4} = 3.25; 3.25 < 3.29$

Maxine received more snow. $3\frac{1}{4}$ is the same as 3.25, and 3.29 is greater than 3.25.

Spectrum Critical Thinking for Math
Grade 5

Chapter 4
Check What You Learned
47

Page 48

NAME _____

🔍 **Check What You Know**

Operations with Fractions

Add or subtract. Write answers in simplest form. Show your work.

1. $\frac{3}{8} + \frac{1}{8} = \frac{4}{8} = \frac{1}{2}$

2. $4\frac{1}{2} + 1\frac{1}{3} = 5\frac{5}{6}$
$4\frac{3}{6} + 1\frac{2}{6} = 5\frac{5}{6}$

3. $3\frac{3}{8} - 1\frac{2}{3} = 1\frac{17}{24}$
$3\frac{9}{24} - 1\frac{16}{24} = 2\frac{33}{24} - 1\frac{16}{24} = 1\frac{17}{24}$

4. $\frac{9}{10} - \frac{3}{10} = \frac{6}{10} = \frac{3}{5}$

Multiply or divide. Write answers in simplest form. Show your work.

5. $\frac{1}{3} \times \frac{4}{5} = \frac{4}{15}$

6. $1\frac{5}{6} \times 2\frac{3}{4} = 5\frac{1}{24}$
$\frac{11}{6} \times \frac{11}{4} = \frac{121}{24}$
$121 \div 24 = 5\frac{1}{24}$

7. $\frac{3}{8} \div 3 = \frac{1}{8}$

8. $4 \div \frac{1}{6} = 24$

Spectrum Critical Thinking for Math
Grade 5
48

Chapter 5
Check What You Know

Answer Key

Page 49

🔍 **Check What You Know**

Operations with Fractions

Solve each problem. Show your work.

9. Sarah made fruit salad for a party. She added $2\frac{1}{2}$ cups of grapes, 4 cups of watermelon, $\frac{3}{4}$ cup of blueberries, and $3\frac{1}{3}$ cups of pineapple. She set aside $1\frac{1}{2}$ cups of fruit salad to eat. How much is left for the party?

$2\frac{1}{2} + 4 + \frac{3}{4} + 3\frac{1}{3} = ?$

$2\frac{6}{12} + 4 + \frac{9}{12} + 3\frac{4}{12} = 9\frac{19}{12}$

$9\frac{19}{12} = 10\frac{7}{12} - 1\frac{1}{2} =$

$10\frac{7}{12} - 1\frac{6}{12} = 9\frac{1}{12}$ cups

10. Paul, Stephanie, Kayla, and Ned went on a road trip. The trip was 140 miles. Paul drove $\frac{1}{2}$ of the way, and Stephanie drove $\frac{1}{4}$ of the way. Kayla and Ned split the rest of the driving equally. How far did Ned drive?

$\frac{1}{2} + \frac{1}{4} = \frac{2}{4} + \frac{1}{4} = \frac{3}{4}$

$140 \times \frac{3}{4} = \frac{420}{4} = 105$

$140 - 105 = 35$

$\begin{array}{r} 17.5 \\ 2)\overline{35.0} \\ -2 \\ \hline 15 \\ -14 \\ \hline 10 \\ -10 \\ \hline 0 \end{array}$

17.5 or $17\frac{1}{2}$ miles

Page 50

Lesson 5.1 Adding with Like Denominators

Adding fractions with like denominators is simple because the fractions represent equal portions. For example, the fifths in the squares below are equal portions. So, the denominator does not change when the two fractions are added together.

$\frac{1}{5} + \frac{2}{5} = \frac{1+2}{5} = \frac{3}{5}$

Use the same strategy to add mixed numbers with like denominators.

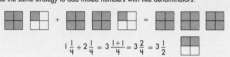

$1\frac{1}{4} + 2\frac{1}{4} = 3\frac{1+1}{4} = 3\frac{2}{4} = 3\frac{1}{2}$

Illustrate and add. Make sure the sum is in simplest form.

$\frac{1}{3} + 4\frac{1}{3} = 4\frac{2}{3}$

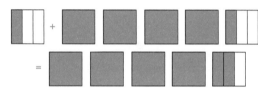

Page 51

Lesson 5.2 Subtracting with Like Denominators

Use the same approach for subtracting fractions with like denominators as you do for adding.

$\frac{5}{6} - \frac{2}{6} = \frac{5-2}{6} = \frac{3}{6} = \frac{1}{2}$

If regrouping is needed, use the denominator for the base.

$4\frac{3}{8} - 1\frac{7}{8} = 3\frac{11}{8} - 1\frac{7}{8} = 2\frac{4}{8} = 2\frac{1}{2}$

Illustrate and subtract. Make sure the difference is in simplest form.

$9\frac{1}{5} - 3\frac{4}{5} =$ _____ $8\frac{6}{5} - 3\frac{4}{5} = 5\frac{2}{5}$

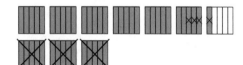

Page 52

Lesson 5.3 Adding with Unlike Denominators

To add fractions or mixed numbers with unlike denominators, use the least common multiple to find a denominator that represents equal portions. Then, create equivalent fractions. Finally, add the fractions or mixed numbers. If needed, convert to a mixed number or put in simplest form.

$\frac{5}{8} + \frac{3}{4} = \frac{5}{8} + \frac{6}{8} = \frac{11}{8} = 1\frac{3}{8}$

Add. If needed, convert the sum to a mixed number or put it in simplest form.

$4\frac{1}{2} + 2\frac{1}{3} =$

$4\frac{3}{6} + 2\frac{2}{6} = 6\frac{5}{6}$

$3\frac{4}{5} + 2\frac{7}{10} =$

$3\frac{8}{10} + 2\frac{7}{10} = 5\frac{15}{10} = 6\frac{5}{10} = 6\frac{1}{2}$

Page 53

NAME _____

Lesson 5.4 Subtracting with Unlike Denominators

To subtract fractions or mixed numbers with unlike denominators, use the least common multiple to find a denominator that represents equal portions. Then, create equivalent fractions. Finally, subtract the fractions or mixed numbers. If needed, convert to a mixed number or put in simplest form.

$$3\frac{5}{6} - \frac{1}{12} = 3\frac{10}{12} - \frac{1}{12} = 3\frac{9}{12} = 3\frac{3}{4}$$

Subtract. Put the difference in simplest form.

$$5\frac{1}{2} - 3\frac{1}{3} =$$

$$5\frac{3}{6} - 3\frac{2}{6} = 2\frac{1}{6}$$

$$7\frac{3}{8} - 2\frac{5}{6} =$$

$$7\frac{18}{48} - \frac{40}{48} = 7\frac{9}{24} - 2\frac{20}{24} = 6\frac{33}{24} - 2\frac{20}{24} = 4\frac{13}{24}$$

Page 54

NAME _____

Lesson 5.5 Multiplying with Models

When whole numbers are multiplied, the product is greater than either of the factors. When fractions are multiplied, the product is usually less than the factors.

To illustrate multiplying fractions, draw a picture showing the first factor. Then, draw a picture showing the other fraction. Lay the two drawings on top of each other to see the product.

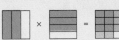  $\frac{2}{3} \times \frac{3}{4} = \frac{6}{12} = \frac{1}{2}$

Draw models to illustrate and solve the multiplication problems.

$$\frac{4}{5} \times \frac{7}{8} = \frac{28}{40} = \frac{7}{10}$$

$$1\frac{1}{2} \times \frac{4}{5} = \frac{3}{2} \times \frac{4}{5} = \frac{12}{10} = 1\frac{2}{10} = 1\frac{1}{5}$$

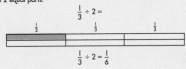

Page 55

NAME _____

Lesson 5.6 Multiplying with Rules

To multiply fractions using rules, multiply the numerators. Then, multiply the denominators. If the fractions are mixed numbers, change them into improper fractions before multiplying. Then, if needed, convert the product back into a mixed number.

$$\frac{3}{4} \times \frac{1}{8} = \frac{3 \times 1}{4 \times 8} = \frac{3}{32} \qquad 2\frac{1}{3} \times 1\frac{1}{2} = \frac{7}{3} \times \frac{3}{2} = \frac{7 \times 3}{3 \times 2} = \frac{21}{6} = 3\frac{3}{6} = 3\frac{1}{2}$$

Show how to solve each problem using a model and using the rule for multiplying fractions.

$$\frac{2}{5} \times \frac{5}{6} = \frac{2 \times 5}{5 \times 6} = \frac{10}{30} = \frac{1}{3}$$

$$3\frac{1}{4} \times \frac{1}{2} = \frac{13}{4} \times \frac{1}{2} = \frac{13}{8} = 1\frac{5}{8}$$

Page 56

NAME _____

Lesson 5.7 Dividing Unit Fractions by Whole Numbers

A unit fraction is any fraction with 1 as the numerator, such as $\frac{1}{2}$ or $\frac{1}{3}$.

When you divide a unit fraction by a whole number, the whole number splits the fraction into smaller portions. On the fraction bar below, the whole number splits each $\frac{1}{3}$ in 2 equal parts.

$$\frac{1}{3} \div 2 =$$

| $\frac{1}{3}$ | $\frac{1}{3}$ | $\frac{1}{3}$ |

$$\frac{1}{3} \div 2 = \frac{1}{6}$$

Draw fraction bars to divide the unit fractions by whole numbers.

$$\frac{1}{4} \div 3 = \frac{1}{12}$$

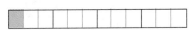

$$\frac{1}{2} \div 5 = \frac{1}{10}$$

Page 57

NAME _____

Lesson 5.8 Dividing Whole Numbers by Unit Fractions

To divide a whole number by a unit fraction, draw out the whole numbers first. Then, split each of them into the number given by the divisor, or unit fraction. Then, count up the total number of portions the whole numbers are split into.

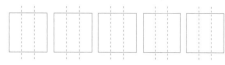

$3 \div \frac{1}{4} = 12$

Illustrate to find the quotient of the division problems below.

$5 \div \frac{1}{3} = 15$

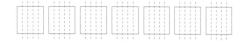

$7 \div \frac{1}{5} = 35$

Page 58

NAME _____

Lesson 5.9 Fraction Operations in the Real World

Tell which operation should be used to solve the real-world problem. Then, solve the problem using a strategy from this chapter.

Nathan ate $\frac{1}{4}$ of a box of cereal for breakfast and his sister ate $\frac{1}{6}$ of it. How much of the cereal did they eat together?

Operation to use: __addition__

$\frac{1}{4} + \frac{1}{6} = \frac{3}{12} + \frac{2}{12} = \frac{5}{12}$

They ate $\frac{5}{12}$ of a box of cereal.

The Smith family had pizza for dinner last night. There is $\frac{1}{8}$ of a pizza left. If Mom eats $\frac{1}{2}$ of what is left for lunch, how much of the total pizza did she eat for lunch?

Operation to use: __multiplication__

$\frac{1}{8} \times \frac{1}{2} = \frac{1 \times 1}{8 \times 2} = \frac{1}{16}$

Mom ate $\frac{1}{16}$ of the pizza.

A bag of cat food contains 10 cups of food. If a cat eats $\frac{1}{4}$ of a cup each day, how long will the bag of cat food last?

Operation to use: __division__

$10 \div \frac{1}{4} = 40$

The cat food will last 40 days.

Page 59

NAME _____

Check What You Learned

Operations with Fractions

Add or subtract. Put your answer in simplest form.

1. $\frac{3}{7} + \frac{3}{8} =$

$\frac{24}{56} + \frac{21}{56} = \frac{45}{56}$

2. $5\frac{1}{6} - 2\frac{1}{3} =$

$\frac{31}{6} - \frac{7}{3} = \frac{31}{6} - \frac{14}{6} = \frac{17}{6} = 2\frac{5}{6}$

Multiply or divide using models. Show your work.

3. $\frac{2}{3} \times \frac{7}{10} = \frac{14}{30} = \frac{7}{15}$

4. $9 \div \frac{1}{3} = 27$

CHAPTER 5 POSTTEST

Page 60

NAME _____

Check What You Learned

Operations with Fractions

Illustrate and divide. Put your answers in simplest form.

5. $\frac{1}{4} \div 5 = \frac{1}{20}$

6. $2 \div \frac{1}{8} = 16$

Tell which operation should be used to solve the real-world problem. Then, solve the problem using rules.

7. Ronald lives $4\frac{2}{3}$ miles from school and Francis lives $2\frac{3}{5}$ miles from school. How much closer does Francis live?

Operation to use: __subtraction__

$4\frac{2}{3} - 2\frac{3}{5} = \frac{14}{3} - \frac{13}{5} = \frac{70}{15} - \frac{39}{15} = \frac{31}{15} = 2\frac{1}{15}$

Francis lives $2\frac{1}{15}$ miles closer to school.

CHAPTER 5 POSTTEST

Page 61

Mid-Test Chapters 1–5

Multiply using the standard method.

1.
$$\begin{array}{r} 8762 \\ \times\quad 64 \\ \hline 35048 \\ +\ 525720 \\ \hline 560{,}768 \end{array}$$

2.
$$\begin{array}{r} 2643 \\ \times\quad 89 \\ \hline 23787 \\ +\ 211440 \\ \hline 235{,}227 \end{array}$$

Divide using an area model.

3. $1{,}984 \div 32 = \underline{62}$

	32	
50	1600	
10	320	
2	64	

$$\begin{array}{r} 1984 \\ -1600 \\ \hline 384 \\ -320 \\ \hline 64 \\ -64 \\ \hline 0 \end{array}$$

$50 + 10 + 2 = 62$

Divide using long division.

4. $72\overline{)11736}$ 163
$$\begin{array}{r} 163 \\ 72\overline{)11736} \\ -72 \\ \hline 453 \\ -432 \\ \hline 216 \\ -216 \\ \hline 0 \end{array}$$

5. $34\overline{)8976}$ 264
$$\begin{array}{r} 264 \\ 34\overline{)8976} \\ -68 \\ \hline 217 \\ -204 \\ \hline 136 \\ -136 \\ \hline 0 \end{array}$$

Page 62

Mid-Test Chapters 1–5

Follow the directions for the number.

3,183

6. Write the value of the underlined digit.

<u>hundreds</u>

7. Write the number in expanded form.

<u>3,000 + 100 + 80 + 3</u>

8. Round the number to the underlined digit.

<u>3,200</u>

9. Write the rounded number as a power of ten to the ones place.

<u>3×10^3</u>

Write the missing value.

10. $6{,}449{,}472 = 6{,}000{,}000 + \underline{400{,}000} + 40{,}000 + 9{,}000 + 400 + 70 + 2$

11. Write these numbers in order on the number line: 3.27, 3.72, 3.072, 3.07.

```
        3.072
  •———•—•————•———————————•————————→
  3  3.07 3.27          3.72      4
```

Page 63

Mid-Test Chapters 1–5

Round each pair of numbers to the underlined digit. Then, compare using <, >, or =.

12. 3,482.13; 3,494.98

  <u>3,500</u> $>$ <u>3,490</u>

13. 467.35; 467.476

  <u>467.4</u> $<$ <u>467.48</u>

14. Multiply using rules: $3{,}729.1 \times 8.75$
$$\begin{array}{r} 3729.1 \\ \times\quad 8.75 \\ \hline 186455 \\ 2610370 \\ +\ 29832800 \\ \hline 32{,}629.625 \end{array}$$

15. Divide using models: $\dfrac{3.6}{12} = 0.3$

```
 1 2 3  4  5 6  7 8 9 10 11 12
[||||][||||][||||][||| ]
```

Convert the improper fraction to a mixed number. Convert the mixed number to a fraction. Show your work.

16. $\dfrac{67}{12} = 5\dfrac{7}{12}$ $67 \div 12 = 5\ R7$

17. $3\dfrac{8}{9} = \dfrac{35}{9}$ $3 \times 9 + 8 = 35$

Page 64

Mid-Test Chapters 1–5

Put the following fractions in order from least to greatest. Illustrate to show your work.

18. $\dfrac{2}{3},\ \dfrac{5}{6},\ \dfrac{3}{4}$ $\dfrac{2}{3},\ \dfrac{3}{4},\ \dfrac{5}{6}$

Solve the problem. Show your work.

19. Travis started a lawn care business. He charged $7.25 per hour for mowing, $13.25 per hour for pulling weeds, and $4.50 per hour for trimming bushes. In July, Travis spent 20 hours mowing, 10 hours pulling weeds, and 3 hours trimming bushes. In August, he spent 25 hours mowing, 5 hours pulling weeds, and $4\frac{1}{2}$ hours trimming bushes. In which month did he make more money?

July	August
$7.25 × 20 = $145.00	$7.25 × 25 = $181.25
$13.25 × 10 = $132.50	$13.25 × 5 = $66.25
$4.50 × 3 = <u>$13.50</u>	$4.50 × $4\frac{1}{2}$ = <u>$20.25</u>
$291.00	$267.75

He made more money in July because $291.00 is greater than $267.75.

Answer Key

Page 65

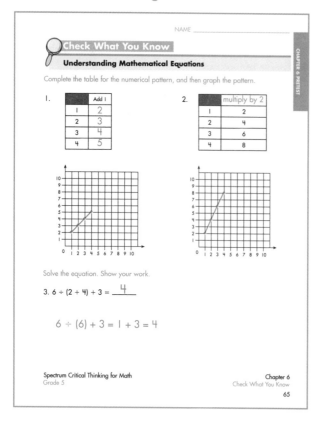

NAME _____

Check What You Know

Understanding Mathematical Equations

Complete the table for the numerical pattern, and then graph the pattern.

1.

	Add 1
1	2
2	3
3	4
4	5

2.

	multiply by 2
1	2
2	4
3	6
4	8

Solve the equation. Show your work.

3. $6 \div (2 + 4) + 3 =$ __4__

$6 \div (6) + 3 = 1 + 3 = 4$

Page 66

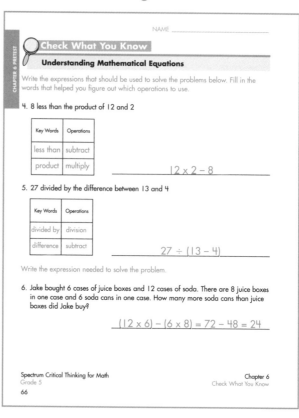

Check What You Know

Understanding Mathematical Equations

Write the expressions that should be used to solve the problems below. Fill in the words that helped you figure out which operations to use.

4. 8 less than the product of 12 and 2

Key Words	Operations
less than	subtract
product	multiply

$12 \times 2 - 8$

5. 27 divided by the difference between 13 and 4

Key Words	Operations
divided by	division
difference	subtract

$27 \div (13 - 4)$

Write the expression needed to solve the problem.

6. Jake bought 6 cases of juice boxes and 12 cases of soda. There are 8 juice boxes in one case and 6 soda cans in one case. How many more soda cans than juice boxes did Jake buy?

$(12 \times 6) - (6 \times 8) = 72 - 48 = 24$

Page 67

NAME _____

Lesson 6.1 Generating Number Patterns

You can use rules to generate a number pattern. For the first pattern, add 1 to each number in the middle column. For the second pattern, add 2 to each number on the left.

	Add 1	Add 2
14	15	16
15	16	17
16	17	18
17	18	19

Use the rules given to generate number patterns.

	Multiply by 2	Multiply by 3
20	40	60
25	50	75
30	60	90
35	70	105

	Add 4	Add 8
16	20	24
20	24	28
24	28	32
28	32	36

	Subtract 5	Subtract 10
35	30	25
40	35	30
45	40	35
50	45	40

	Divide by 2	Divide by 3
6	3	2
12	6	4
18	9	6
24	12	8

Page 68

NAME _____

Lesson 6.2 Identifying Number Patterns

You can examine the relationships between numbers in a pattern to find the rule used to create the pattern.

	Add 2	Add 4
12	14	16
14	16	18
16	18	20
18	20	22

Use the numbers given to find the rule used to complete the pattern. Explain your answer.

	multiply by 3	multiply by 5
9	27	45
12	36	60
15	45	75
18	54	90

Explain: __Answer found by discovering that each number in the first column was a factor of the numbers in the other columns.__

	divide by 2	divide by 4
4	2	1
8	4	2
12	6	3
16	8	4

Explain: __Answer found by discovering that each number in the first column was a multiple of the numbers in the other columns.__

Answer Key

Page 69

NAME

Lesson 6.3 Graphing Number Patterns

When a mathematical pattern exists, you can graph it on a coordinate grid to understand the relationship between the numbers.

	Add 3
1	4
2	5
3	6
4	7

Each pair of numbers makes an ordered pair:
(1, 4), (2, 5), (3, 6), (4, 7)

Complete the pattern table below. Then, graph the pattern.

	Multiply by 2
1	2
2	4
3	6
4	8

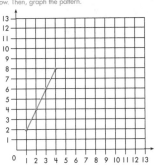

Spectrum Critical Thinking for Math
Grade 5

Lesson 6.3
Graphing Number Patterns
69

Page 70

NAME

Lesson 6.4 Order of Operations

The **order of operations** is used to find the value of an expression with more than one kind of operation.

1. Do all operations within parentheses, braces, or brackets.
2. Do all multiplication and division in order, from left to right.
3. Do all addition and subtraction in order, from left to right.

$36 \div (11 + 3 - 2) + 2$	Do operations inside parentheses, braces, or brackets.
$36 \div 12 + 2$	Multiply and divide from left to right.
$3 + 2$	Add and subtract from left to right.
5	

Use complete sentences to explain the order of operations needed for each problem. Then, solve.

Kate has $300. She spends $150 on food. She spends half of what she has left on clothes. Then, she finds $24 more in a coat pocket. How much money does Kate have left?

First, subtract $150 from $300 and divide the difference by 2. Then, add 24 to the quotient. Answer: $99

Marvin bought 3 packs of pencils for $1.50 each, 2 packs of markers for $3.25 each, and 5 notebooks for $0.99 each. If Marvin started with $35, how much does he have left?

First, multiply the number of each item by the cost of the item. Then, add each of those products together. Subtract the sum from $35. Answer: $19.05

Spectrum Critical Thinking for Math
Grade 5
70

Lesson 6.4
Order of Operations

Page 71

NAME

Lesson 6.5 Simple Expressions

Key words can help you write simple expressions to solve word problems. The tables below show some key words.

Key Words	Operation
more than	addition
less than	subtraction
difference	subtraction

Key Words	Operation
times	multiplication
half	division
divided by	division

Write a simple expression for each problem. Then, solve each problem using order of operations.

Tom is 6 inches shorter than Pete, who is 8 inches taller than Jerry. If Tom is 64 inches tall, how tall is Jerry?

Expression: Jerry = 64 + 6 − 8   Answer: 62 inches

The grocery store has 4 times the number of apples as it does oranges. If the grocery store has 17 oranges, how many apples does the grocery store have?

Expression: Apples = 17 × 4   Answer: 68 apples

Meredith scored the highest grade on the math test with a 98. Jeremy scored 6 points less than Meredith. Suzanne received half of Jeremy's score. What did Suzanne score on her test?

Expression: Suzanne = (98 − 6) ÷ 2   Answer: 46

Spectrum Critical Thinking for Math
Grade 5

Lesson 6.5
Simple Expressions
71

Page 72

NAME

Lesson 6.6 Equations in the Real World

Review the problem structures for math operations.

Add or Subtract	Multiply or Divide
add to or take from	equal groups
put together or take apart	arrays
compare	compare

Create an equation to answer each question. Then, solve.

Ticket prices to the zoo are $10 for adults and $7 for children. Teachers get in for free. There are 130 fifth-grade students and 5 teachers. If the zoo requires 1 adult to attend for every 10 students, how many adults will need to attend in addition to the 5 teachers?

Expression: Number of adults who need tickets: 130 ÷ 10 − 5

Solution: 8 adults

How much will the trip to the zoo cost?

Expression: Cost of field trip: ($10 × 8) + ($7 × 130)

Solution: $990

Explain how you calculated the total cost of adult tickets.

You only have to buy 8 tickets for adults because the 5 teachers will get in free.

Spectrum Critical Thinking for Math
Grade 5
72

Lesson 6.6
Equations in the Real World

Answer Key

Page 73

💡 Check What You Learned
Understanding Mathematical Equations

Complete the table for the numerical pattern. Then, graph the pattern.

1.

	Add 5
1	6
2	7
3	8
4	9

2.

	÷ 3
3	1
6	2
9	3
12	4

Solve the equation. Show your work. Then, list the operations you used in order.

3. $42 ÷ (6 + 1) × 2 =$ _____

$42 ÷ 7 × 2$
$6 × 2$
12

a) _addition_
b) _division_
c) _multiplication_

Page 74

💡 Check What You Learned
Understanding Mathematical Equations

Create an equation to solve this real-world problem. Then, solve and explain the clues you used.

4. Olivia is playing a video game. She hits 10 bonuses that are worth 250 points each. Every time she passes a level, she gets a 500-point bonus. Her base scores are 150 on level 1, 275 on level 2, 330 on level 3, and 355 on level 4. If the high score on the video game is 7,200, how many points will she need to reach the high score when she passes level 5?

Equation: $7,200 − (10 × 250) − (5 × 500) − (150 + 275 + 330 + 355) =$

Solution: _1,090_

Explanation: To find out how many points Olivia needs, subtract all of the points she has earned so far and her bonus for passing level 5 from the high score.

Page 75

🔍 Check What You Know
Measurement

Convert the measurements below.

1. 27 feet = _9_ yards

2. 1,000 centimeters = _10_ meters

3. 5,600 grams = _560,000_ centigrams

4. 80 ounces = _5_ pounds

Create a line plot to show the situation. Then, solve the problem.

5. A group of friends meet at a restaurant. Fred places an order for 5 chicken wings. Mike and Tony each place an order for 8 wings. John, Jake, and Jim order 10 wings each. Al orders 12 wings. How many wings did they order in all?

$5 + (2 × 8) + (3 × 10) + 12$
$5 + 16 + 30 + 12$
63 wings

Fill in the missing numbers. Then, find the perimeter and area of the shape. Show your work.

6.

$P =$ _26_ m

$A =$ _33_ m²

$P = 4 + 3 + 3 + 3 + 7 + 6$
$A = (3 × 3) + (4 × 6)$

Page 76

🔍 Check What You Know
Measurement

Find the volume of the figure below. Explain how you got your answer.

7.

3 cm
5 cm
3 cm

$V =$ _45 cm³_

Multiply base times height times width: $3 × 5 = 15$;
$15 × 3 = 45$

Solve the word problems. Show your work.

8. Joan needs to buy new carpet for the two bedrooms in her house. The bedrooms are 12 feet by 10 feet and 15 feet by 18 feet. How many square feet of carpet does Joan need to buy?

$(12 × 10) + (15 × 18) = 390$ square feet

9. The new fish tank is 28 inches long, 12 inches high, and 16 inches deep. How many cubic inches of water will it take to fill the tank?

$28 × 12 × 16 = 5,376$ cubic inches

Page 77

NAME _____

Lesson 7.1 Standard Measurement Conversions

Length	Volume	Weight
1 mile (mi.) = 1,760 yards (yd.)	1 gallon (gal.) = 4 quarts (qt.)	
1 mile (mi.) = 5,280 feet (ft.)	1 gallon (gal.) = 8 pints (pt.)	1 pound (lb.) = 16 ounces (oz.)
1 yard (yd.) = 36 inches (in.)	1 quart (qt.) = 2 pints (pt.)	
1 yard (yd.) = 3 feet (ft.)	1 quart (qt.) = 4 cups (c.)	2,000 pounds (lb.) = 1 ton (T.)
1 foot (ft.) = 12 inches (in.)	1 pint (pt.) = 2 cups (c.)	

Solve the measurement problems using the conversion table. Show your work.

A football field is 100 yards long. If Mike throws the football 273 feet from one end of the field, how many more yards is it to the other end of the field?

$$100 \text{ yards} = 300 \text{ feet}, \ 300 - 273 = 27 \text{ feet}$$
$$27 \div 3 = 9 \text{ yards}$$

Marissa needs 1 gallon of iced tea for the cookout. She has 8 cups already. If she is making the tea in a 1-pint pitcher, how many pints does she need to make?

$$1 \text{ gallon} = 16 \text{ cups} = 8 \text{ pints}; \ 16 - 8 = 8 \text{ cups};$$
$$8 \text{ cups} = 4 \text{ pints}$$

A truck has a capacity of 2 tons. If the truck is already loaded with 3,587 pounds of coal, how many more pounds can it hold?

$$2 \text{ tons} = 4,000 \text{ pounds}; \ 4,000 - 3,587 = 413 \text{ pounds}$$

Page 78

NAME _____

Lesson 7.2 Metric Measurement Conversions

Length	Weight	Volume
1 kilometer (k) = 1,000 meters (m)	1 kilogram (kg) = 1,000 grams (g)	1 kiloliter (kL) = 1,000 liters (L)
1 meter (m) = 0.001 kilometers (km)	1 gram (g) = 0.001 kilograms (kg)	1 liter (L) = 0.001 kiloliters (kL)
1 meter (m) = 100 centimeters (cm)	1 gram (g) = 100 centigrams (cg)	1 liter (L) = 100 centiliters (cL)
1 centimeter (cm) = 0.01 meters (m)	1 centigram (cg) = 0.01 grams (g)	1 centiliter (cL) = 0.01 liters (L)
1 meter (m) = 1,000 millimeters (mm)	1 gram (g) = 1,000 milligrams (mg)	1 liter (L) = 1,000 milliliters (mL)
1 millimeter (mm) = 0.001 meter (m)	1 milligram (mg) = 0.001 gram (g)	1 milliliter (mL) = 0.001 liters (L)

Solve the measurement problems using the conversion table. Show your work.

The bulletin board for the classroom is 5 meters long. Ms. Jones has 190 centimeters of fabric to cover the board. How much more fabric is needed?

$$5 \text{ meters} = 500 \text{ centimeters}; \ 500 - 190 = 310 \text{ centimeters}$$

A paper clip weighs about 1 gram. If 100 paper clips come in a box, how many boxes of paper clips will be needed to make the weight of one kilogram?

$$100 \text{ paper clips} = 100 \text{ grams}; \ 1 \text{ kilogram} = 1,000 \text{ grams};$$
$$1,000 \div 100 = 10 \text{ boxes}$$

The science experiment requires 4 centiliters of vinegar. If the vinegar bottle has 1.5 liters in it, how many centiliters will be left after the experiment?

$$1.5 \text{ liters} = 150 \text{ centiliters}; \ 150 - 4 = 146 \text{ centiliters}$$

Page 79

NAME _____

Lesson 7.3 Using Line Plots to Solve Problems

A **line plot** is used to mark how many times something occurs in a data set. Line plots can help organize information to solve problems.

A pitcher holds 3 quarts of punch. There are several glasses being filled from the pitcher that hold various amounts: 3 glasses hold $\frac{1}{8}$ qt., 2 glasses hold $\frac{1}{4}$ qt., and 5 glasses hold $\frac{1}{3}$ qt. How much punch will be left in the pitcher after all the glasses are filled?

$$3 - [(3 \times \tfrac{1}{8}) + (2 \times \tfrac{1}{4}) + (5 \times \tfrac{1}{3})] =$$
$$3 - (\tfrac{3}{8} + \tfrac{2}{4} + \tfrac{5}{3}) = 3 - (\tfrac{9}{24} + \tfrac{12}{24} + \tfrac{40}{24}) =$$
$$\tfrac{72}{24} - \tfrac{61}{24} = \tfrac{11}{24} \text{ qt.}$$

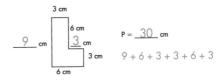

Create a line plot to answer the question. Show your work and explain your answer.

Kendra and her friends buy gummy worms at the candy store. Kendra buys $\frac{1}{3}$ pound of gummy worms. Two of her friends buy $\frac{1}{4}$ pound each, and three other friends buy $\frac{1}{2}$ pound each. The store offers a discount for buying 3 pounds or more of candy. Do Kendra and her friends qualify for the discount?

$$\tfrac{1}{3} + (2 \times \tfrac{1}{4}) + (3 \times \tfrac{1}{2}) =$$
$$\tfrac{1}{3} + \tfrac{2}{4} + \tfrac{3}{2} = \tfrac{1}{3} + \tfrac{1}{2} + \tfrac{3}{2} =$$
$$\tfrac{2}{6} + \tfrac{3}{6} + \tfrac{9}{6} = \tfrac{14}{6} = 2\tfrac{2}{6} = 2\tfrac{1}{3}$$

Kendra and her friends will not get the discount. They bought $2\frac{1}{3}$ pounds of gummy worms, which is less than 3 pounds.

Page 80

NAME _____

Lesson 7.4 Perimeter of Irregular Shapes

To find the perimeter of an irregular shape, find the lengths of all the sides and add them together.

$$5 + 1 + 1 + 3 + 1 + 1 + 5 + 1 + 1 + 3 + 1 + 1 =$$
$$24 \text{ inches}$$

Fill in the missing numbers. Then, find the perimeter of each shape. Show your work.

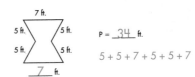

P = __30__ cm

$$9 + 6 + 3 + 3 + 6 + 3$$

P = __34__ ft.

$$5 + 5 + 7 + 5 + 5 + 7$$

Answer Key

Page 81

NAME _____

Lesson 7.5 Area of Irregular Shapes

To find the area of an irregular polygon, decompose to create simple polygons. Then, add the area of each simple polygon together.

Polygon 1 = 8 ft. × 6 ft. = 48 square feet

Polygon 2 = 2 ft. × 2 ft. = 4 square feet

Polygon area = 48 square feet + 4 square feet

Polygon area = 52 square feet

Decompose the irregular polygon to find its area. Show your work. Use lines to show how the polygon was decomposed.

A = __80__ in.²

$(4 \times 4) + (4 \times 4) + (4 \times 4) + (4 \times 4) + (4 \times 4)$

Show two different ways to decompose the irregular polygon. Then, find the area both ways.

A = __29__ in.²

$(6 \times 3) + (2 \times 3) + (1 \times 5)$

or

$(3 \times 3) + (6 \times 3) + (2 \times 1)$

Spectrum Critical Thinking for Math
Grade 5

Lesson 7.5
Area of Irregular Shapes
81

Page 82

NAME _____

Lesson 7.6 Calculating Volume with Unit Cubes

You can find the volume of a rectangular solid by figuring out how many cubes of a particular unit size will fit inside the shape.

First, divide the figure into given length units.

Next, divide the figure into given height units.

Last, divide the figure into given width units.

$5 \times 5 \times 5 = 125$

Illustrate and multiply to find the volume of the rectangular solids.

__7__ × __3__ × __9__ = __189__ cubic ft.

__9__ × __2__ × __8__ = __144__ cubic cm

Spectrum Critical Thinking for Math
Grade 5
82

Lesson 7.6
Calculating Volume with Unit Cubes

Page 83

NAME _____

Lesson 7.7 Calculating Volume with Multiplication

To find the volume of a rectangular solid, you can multiply the length, height, and width.

Volume = length × width × height

Volume = 6 ft. × 3 ft. × 5 ft.

Volume = 90 cubic feet

A produce shipping crate for grapefruit is 9 feet long, 7 feet tall, and 2 feet wide. What is the volume of the shipping crate?

7 × 2 × 9 = 126 cubic feet

A yard waste bin is 4 feet long, 5 feet tall, and 3 feet deep. What is the volume of the yard waste bin?

5 × 4 × 3 = 60 cubic feet

Spectrum Critical Thinking for Math
Grade 5

Lesson 7.7
Calculating Volume with Multiplication
83

Page 84

NAME _____

Lesson 7.8 Measurement in the Real World

Solve each problem and show your work.

Gabriel is making punch for a cookout. The recipe he is using makes 28 cups of punch. Gabriel has 1-quart pitchers for serving the punch. How many pitchers will he need?

1 quart = 4 cups; 28 ÷ 4 = 7; 7 one-quart pitchers are needed

Melissa bought a poster that is 19 inches wide and 24 inches tall. If she wants to frame the poster, how much framing material will she need?

19 + 19 + 24 + 24 = 86 inches of framing material

The toy factory ships toys in crates that are 2 feet wide, 6 feet long, and 3 feet high. If each toy is 1 foot wide, 2 feet long, and 1 foot high, how many toys can go into each crate?

2 × 6 × 3 = 36 cubic feet; 36 ÷ 2 = 18 toys

Spectrum Critical Thinking for Math
Grade 5
84

Lesson 7.8
Measurement in the Real World

Page 85

Check What You Learned

Measurement

Convert the measurements below. Show your work.

1. 64 cups = __4__ gallons

2. 450 meters = __0.45__ kilometers

Create a line plot to show the situation. Then, solve the problem.

3. Meg wants to try some new chocolate chip cookie recipes. The recipes call for different amounts of sugar. 2 recipes call for $\frac{1}{2}$ cup of sugar. 3 recipes call for $\frac{3}{4}$ cup of sugar. 3 recipes call for $\frac{1}{3}$ cup of sugar. How much sugar does Meg need to make all of the recipes?

$(2 \times \frac{1}{2}) + (3 \times \frac{3}{4}) + (3 \times \frac{1}{3}) =$

$4 \frac{1}{4}$ cups of sugar

Find the perimeter and area of the shape. Show your work.

4.

P = __32__ ft.

A = __52__ ft.^{2}

$P = 8 + 8 + 6 + 6 + 2 + 2$

$A = (2 \times 2) + (6 \times 8)$

Page 86

Check What You Learned

Measurement

Find the volume of the figure below. Show your work.

5.

V = __64__ ft.^{3}

$4 \times 4 \times 4$

Solve the word problems. Show your work.

6. The school wants to put a new fence around the playgrounds. One playground is 25 yards by 50 yards and the other playground is 30 yards by 45 yards. How much fencing does the school need?

$(25 + 25 + 50 + 50) + (30 + 30 + 45 + 45)$

$= 150 + 150 = 300$ yards of fencing

7. A swimming pool is 25 meters long, 15 meters across, and 2 meters deep. How many cubic meters of water will the swimming pool hold?

$25 \times 15 \times 2 = 750$ cubic meters of water

Page 87

Check What You Know

Geometry

Label each of the polygons and name one characteristic of that type of polygon.

1.

Name: __parallelogram__

Characteristic: __2 pairs of__ __parallel sides__

2.

Name: __trapezoid__

Characteristic: __1 pair of__ __parallel sides__

3.

Name: __square__

Characteristic: __4 equal sides__

4.

Name: __pentagon__

Characteristic: __figure with 5__ __sides__

Page 88

Check What You Know

Geometry

Plot each ordered pair on the coordinate grid.

5. A (4, 5)
   B (6, 2)
   C (1, 8)

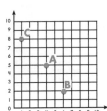

Use the coordinate grid to complete the polygon described. Answer the question and show your work.

6. A square has corners at (5, 5) and (8, 8). What are the perimeter and area of the square?

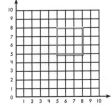

Perimeter = 3 + 3 + 3 + 3 = 12 units

Area = 3 × 3 = 9 square units

Answer Key

Page 89

NAME _____

Lesson 8.1 Understanding Polygons

Every type of polygon has a unique set of characteristics. For example, a square has four equal sides and four 90-degree angles. No other polygon has those exact characteristics.

Use the word bank to fill in each blank. Then, draw the figure described.

rectangle	trapezoid	equilateral triangle

I have three equal sides and my angles add up to 180 degrees.

I am a(n) _equilateral triangle_ .

I have four right angles, two pairs of parallel sides, and two pairs of equal sides.

I am a(n) _rectangle_____ .

I have four sides, but only one set is parallel. My angles add up to 360 degrees.

I am a(n) _trapezoid_____ .

Page 90

NAME _____

Lesson 8.2 Categorizing and Classifying Polygons

Some polygons fit into more than one category. For example, a square is also a rectangle and a quadrilateral because it also fits those characteristics.

polygon
- quadrilateral — parallelogram — rectangle, rhombus — square
- pentagon
- triangle — scalene, isosceles, equilateral
- hexagon
- trapezoid

Use the chart above to complete the statements describing polygons.

All ___squares___ are rectangles, but not all rectangles are ___squares___ .

There are ___3___ types of triangles: ___scalene___ , ___isosceles___ , and _equilateral_ .

acceptable answers: pentagon, triangle, hexagon
A _____ is a type of polygon, but it is not a quadrilateral.

A ___trapezoid___ is a type of quadrilateral that is not a parallelogram.

Page 91

NAME _____

Lesson 8.3 Understanding Coordinate Grids

The x-axis runs on a horizontal line.

The y-axis runs on a vertical line.

Points located on the same grid are called **coordinate points**, or **coordinates**.

A point on a grid is located by using an **ordered pair**. An ordered pair lists the x-axis point first and then the y-axis point.

(10, 3)
(x, y)
1. Count right 10 lines.
2. From that point, go up 3.
3. Draw a point.

Draw arrows to show how to find each ordered pair. Then, mark the spot where the ordered pair is located.

(3, 7)   (8, 4)

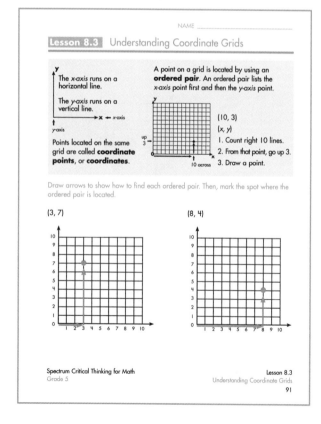

Page 92

NAME _____

Lesson 8.4 Problem Solving with Coordinate Grids

Draw the figures described. Then, solve the problems using the coordinate grid.

A square has corners at (4, 6), (4, 9), (7, 6), and (7, 9). What is the area of the square?

A = ___9___ units²

A polygon has right angles at (3, 1), (3,7), (9,7), (9,4), (6,4), and (6,1). What is the area of the polygon?

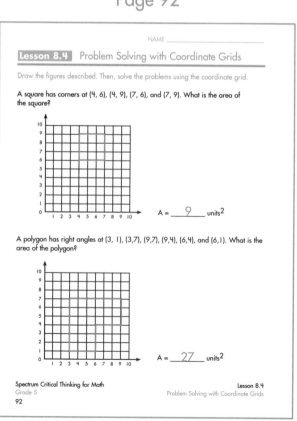

A = ___27___ units²

Page 93

NAME _____

Lesson 8.5 Geometry in the Real World

Solve the problems. Show your work.

An engineer needs to design a support for the beams on a bridge. The support must have 4 corners to distribute the weight evenly and at least one pair of parallel sides so it will be level. The top of the support cannot be wider than the base or overhang the base at any point. What shapes will work as beam supports?

Square, rectangle, trapezoid. These polygons all have 4 corners and at least one pair of parallel sides. A parallelogram won't work because one of the corners would hang beyond the base.

Randy walks from home (2, 8) to school (7, 8) each morning. After school, he stops to meet his friend, Shane, at his house (7, 3). Then, they walk to the library (2, 3) to do their homework. After his homework is finished, Randy walks home. How far does Randy have to walk each day?

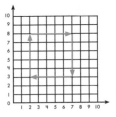

20 units

Spectrum Critical Thinking for Math
Grade 5

Lesson 8.5
Geometry in the Real World
93

Page 94

NAME _____

💡 **Check What You Learned**

Geometry

Complete the statements about polygons.

1. A rhombus is a ___parallelogram___ with ___4___ equal sides.

2. A scalene ___triangle___ has ___3___ sides that are unequal.

3. A(n) ___hexagon___ has 6 sides.

Draw arrows to show how to place ordered pairs on the coordinate grids.

4. (7, 4)   5. (3, 8)

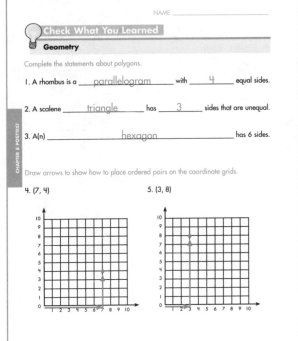

Spectrum Critical Thinking for Math
Grade 5
94

Chapter 8
Check What You Learned

Page 95

NAME _____

💡 **Check What You Learned**

Geometry

Use the blank coordinate grid to solve the problems below.

6. A rectangle has corners at (4,3) and (6,10). What is the perimeter of the rectangle?

Perimeter = 18 units

7. A line runs from (2,2) to (7,2). How long is the line?

5 units

Use the blank coordinate grid to solve the problem.

8. Ginny walks from her house at (3,3) to the park at (8,3). After that, she goes to the grocery store at (8,5), the shoe store at (5,5), and the bank at (5,8). Then, she visits a friend at (3,8) before she walks back home. How far did Ginny walk today?

20 units

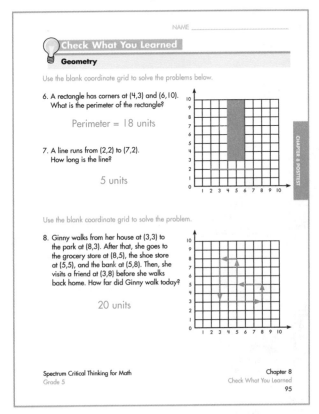

Spectrum Critical Thinking for Math
Grade 5

Chapter 8
Check What You Learned
95

Page 96

NAME _____

Final Test Chapters 1–8

Add, subtract, multiply, or divide using the strategy in parentheses.

1. (standard)
$$\begin{array}{r} 281.21 \\ \times\ 1.2 \\ \hline 56242 \\ +\ 281210 \\ \hline 337.452 \end{array}$$

2. (place value)
$$\begin{array}{r} 8271 \\ \times\ 836 \\ \hline \end{array}$$
$8271 \times 800 = 6616800$
$8271 \times 30 =\ 248130$
$+\ \ 8271 \times 6 =\ \ \ 49626$
$$\overline{\ \ \ 6,914,556}$$

3. (rules) $2.3\overline{)225.4}$

$$\begin{array}{r} 98 \\ 2.3\overline{)2254} \\ -\ 207 \\ \hline 184 \\ -\ 184 \\ \hline 0 \end{array}$$

4. (rules) $\dfrac{3}{4} \times 2\dfrac{1}{3} =$ _____

$\dfrac{3}{4} \times \dfrac{7}{3} = \dfrac{21}{12} = 1\dfrac{9}{12} = 1\dfrac{3}{4}$

5. (models) $8 \div \dfrac{1}{7} =$ ___56___

6. (rules) $\dfrac{6}{7} \times 2\dfrac{3}{14} =$ _____

$\dfrac{6}{7} \times \dfrac{31}{14} = \dfrac{186}{98}$

$= 1\dfrac{88}{98} = 1\dfrac{44}{49}$

Spectrum Critical Thinking for Math
Grade 5
96

Chapters 1–8
Final Test

Page 97

NAME _____

Final Test Chapters 1-8

Complete the number pattern and graph it on the blank coordinate grid.

7.
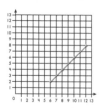

	Subtract 4
6	2
8	4
10	6
12	8

Use order of operations to solve the equations below. Show your work.

8. $13 + (9 \times 2) =$ __31__

$13 + 18 = 31$

9. $(15 - 5) + 2 \times 12 =$ __34__

$10 + 2 \times 12 = 10 + 24 = 34$

Convert the measurements. Show your work.

10. 384 ounces = __24__ pounds

$384 \div 16 = 24$

11. 89 grams = __0.89__ centigrams

$89 \div 100 = 0.89$

Spectrum Critical Thinking for Math
Grade 5

Chapters 1-8
Final Test
97

Page 98

NAME _____

Final Test Chapters 1-8

Find the area.

12.

A = __36__ sq. cm

Area: $(9 \times 3) + (3 \times 3) = 36$ square cm

Fill in the blanks to describe polygons.

13. A square has 4 __equal__ sides and 4 __right__ angles.

14. A trapezoid is a __quadrilateral__ that has __1__ pair(s) of parallel sides and __4__ angles.

15. A __pentagon__ has 5 sides.

Find and label the points on the coordinate grid.

16. A at (3,7)

17. B at (4,3)

18. C at (9,10)

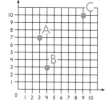

Spectrum Critical Thinking for Math
Grade 5
98

Chapters 1-8
Final Test

Page 99

NAME _____

Final Test Chapters 1-8

Solve the multi-step problem below and show your work.

19. You have a vegetable garden that is 20 feet long and 13 yards and 1 foot wide. You want the dirt to be 2 feet deep. How much dirt will you need?

13 yards 1 foot = 40 feet

$20 \times 40 \times 2 = 1,600$ cubic feet of dirt

What is the area of the entire garden?

800 square feet

$\frac{1}{4}$ of the vegetable garden will be tomatoes, $\frac{1}{6}$ will be carrots, $\frac{1}{8}$ will be peppers, and $\frac{1}{4}$ will be corn. What fraction of the garden's area will those vegetables take up?

$(2 \times \frac{1}{4}) + \frac{1}{6} + \frac{1}{8} = \frac{2}{4} + \frac{1}{6} + \frac{1}{8} =$

$\frac{12}{24} + \frac{4}{24} + \frac{3}{24} = \frac{19}{24}$

What fraction of the garden is unplanted? Draw a picture to illustrate.

tomatoes	carrots		
corn	peppers		

$\frac{5}{24}$ of the garden is unplanted.

Spectrum Critical Thinking for Math
Grade 5

Chapters 1-8
Final Test
99

Page 100

NAME _____

Final Test Chapters 1-8

Solve the multi-step problem below and show your work.

20. You are planning a pizza party. You have permission to invite 24 friends and you have a budget of $100. The pizza place you are ordering from will cut 14-inch pizzas into 8 slices or 12 slices. A cheese pizza costs $7.99, a 1-topping pizza costs $8.99, and a 2-topping pizza costs $10.99.

How many pizzas of each type will you order?

Answers may vary. Possible answer:

12 pizzas - 11 cheese, 1 2-topping, totaling $98.88

How many slices will each guest be able to eat? Explain your answer. Show your work.

Answers may vary. If I order 12 pizzas and each pizza is cut into 12 slices, there will be $12 \times 12 = 144$ slices. Including myself, there will be 25 people. Since $144 \div 25 = 5r19$, each person will get at least 5 slices.

Spectrum Critical Thinking for Math
Grade 5
100

Chapters 1-8
Final Test

Notes

Notes

Notes

Notes